La Maisam

SIMPLIFYING BAKING ONE RECIPE AT A TIME

MAISAM ALGIRGEET

©2025 Maisam Algirgeet and
Meze Publishing Limited
ISBN: 978-1-915538-40-6
Written by: Maisam Algirgeet
Photography by: Ellie Grace
(elliegracephotography.co.uk)
Designed by: Paul Cocker
Sales and PR: Emma Toogood
Proofreading: Katie Fisher
Contributors: Emily Readman
and Heather Treaton

me ze

Published by
Meze Publishing Limited
Unit 1b, 2 Kelham Square
Kelham Riverside
Sheffield S3 8SD
Web: www.mezepublishing.co.uk
Telephone: 0114 275 7709
Email: info@mezepublishing.co.uk

CONTENTS

FOUNDATIONS

CAKES

BISCUITS & COOKIES

ABOUT ME

Hi! I'm Maisam. You might know me from The Great British Bake Off 2022 or maybe from one of my baking videos on Instagram. However you found your way here, I'm so glad you're holding this book.

I was born in a small mountain town in Libya and moved to Manchester when I was nine. I didn't speak a word of English at the time, but little by little, it began to feel like home. Baking came later, and after a phase of trying every hobby under the sun, I fell headfirst into the world of YouTube tutorials and recipe fails (my first cinnamon rolls were basically bricks). But I kept going. I've always been a bit stubborn like that.

Eventually, I built up the courage to apply for Bake Off. I was 18 and never expected to get in... but I did. I became the youngest contestant in my series and that experience changed everything. It showed me that baking could be more than just a hobby. It could be a way to tell stories, connect cultures, and bring people together. I started sharing my bakes online a few years ago, mostly just for fun. At the time, I was studying Interior Design, baking at 2am between deadlines, and uploading recipes for a tiny group of friends and family. I never imagined it would grow into a real community but somehow, it did.

La Maisam started as a small baking page. The name was inspired by Maison, the French word for home – a quiet nod to my name, my love for interiors, and my love for warm, welcoming spaces. I added La to give it a bit of character and the name just stuck. Over time, La Maisam became more than just a name. It's how people came to know my bakes even before they knew me. This little page helped me discover that I had my own style, my own way of baking, and now, a place to share it.

Since then, I've shared hundreds of recipes, connected with bakers around the world, and poured my heart into this first book – a space where we can slow down, bake together, and bring a little more comfort into our kitchens.

This book is everything I needed when I first started baking: recipes that feel approachable, flavours that reflect who I am, and the kind of food that says, you're home. I wrote it for anyone who's ever found joy in baking, and in sharing something you made with your hands.

Whether you've just discovered my bakes or you've been here since the early ciabatta days – welcome, I'm so happy you're here!

Lots of love,

Maisam

INGREDIENT NOTES

This book uses UK measurements and terminology. Here are a few ingredients or terms that might be unfamiliar if you're reading from outside the UK:

Strong white bread flour

This is high-protein white flour (typically 12–14% protein), ideal for breadmaking. In other countries, it may be labelled as bread flour or high-gluten flour.

Plain flour

The UK equivalent of all-purpose flour.

Self-raising flour

Flour with added baking powder – usually around 2 tsp per 150g. If it's not available where you are, you can make your own by combining plain/all-purpose flour with baking powder.

Yeast

I tend to use instant yeast, also called fast-action yeast, which can be mixed straight into the flour. If using active dry yeast, dissolve it in warm liquid first to activate it.

Cornflour

In the UK, this refers to what's known as cornstarch elsewhere – a fine white powder used to thicken custards or to soften cookies.

Double cream

A rich cream with around 48% fat. The closest substitutes are heavy cream or whipping cream – just avoid half-and-half, which won't behave the same way in recipes.

Caster sugar

A fine white sugar, finer than granulated but not as powdery as icing sugar. If you can't find it, you can pulse granulated sugar in a blender to make your own.

Icing sugar

Also known as powdered sugar or confectioners' sugar.

Bicarbonate of soda

Called baking soda in other countries.

Demerara sugar

An unrefined sugar with large crystals and a warm, caramel flavour.

I've tested all the recipes using ingredients that are widely available in the UK. Wherever you're baking, feel free to adapt based on what's accessible to you.

MY FAVOURITE TOOLS

These are the tools that carried me through this book and through years of baking before it. You'll spot them in the background of so many of my videos. They're not fancy. Some are scratched and worn. But they work, and they've earned their place in my kitchen. I've never been a fan of unnecessary gadgets. I like tools that actually help. The ones you reach for without thinking. The ones that make things easier, cleaner, or just feel good in your hand. You don't need a drawer full of kit to bake well, just a few solid tools that do their job properly.

Digital scale

Switching to a scale completely changed my baking. Growing up, my mum (an amazing baker) never used one; she used cups and always said, "you measure with your eyes." I'm the complete opposite! I need precision. I still use the same £5 scale I bought when I was 13, and it's been used for every single recipe in this book. Weighing in grams gives you consistency and accuracy. If I could convince you to get just one thing, it would be a digital scale. It doesn't need to be fancy – mine's bright pink and a little worn, but I use it every single day.

Dough scraper

A total lifesaver if you're making any of the stickier doughs in this book. I use it for shaping, lifting, cutting, and even cleaning down the counter. It's the kind of tool that quickly becomes essential.

Danish dough whisk

A funny-looking tool that makes so much sense once you try it. It mixes dough and thick batters easily without overworking them. I reach for it all the time – especially when I don't want to make a mess or dive straight in with my hands.

Ice cream scoop

My not-so-secret tool for evenly portioned cookies. It helps everything bake evenly and look neat, without much effort. I use it for muffins and cupcakes too – anything that benefits from consistent sizing.

Offset spatula

Small but incredibly useful. I use mine for smoothing batter, lifting cookies and pastries off trays, spreading frosting – it's a quiet hero in my kitchen.

Flour duster

I get asked about this one all the time. It's the little tool I use in nearly every bread video to dust flour onto the work surface. I prefer it to a regular sieve – it gives a softer, more even finish without all the mess. It's also my go-to for dusting icing sugar or cocoa powder on finished bakes.

Microplane grater

Perfect for zesting citrus and grating chocolate or a bit of fresh nutmeg. You'll spot it often in my cake recipes.

Measuring spoons

Everyday essentials are the standard 5ml and 15ml (teaspoon and tablespoon) spoons. I use them constantly, especially when it comes to extracts, spices and raising agents.

5 ml
15 ml
BLADE MADE IN USA
Microplane
SILVERCREST
unit
tara

FOUNDATIONS

The building blocks of baking

This chapter covers the essentials – doughs, batters, and pastry that form the base for recipes throughout the book. Simple, no-stress techniques set the foundation for more advanced bakes later.

NO-KNEAD DOUGH

Making bread from scratch doesn't have to be complicated. This no-knead dough is simple, hands-off, and incredibly versatile. It's one of my most loved recipes and a go-to for thousands of my followers. Whether you're making pizza, focaccia, rolls, or ciabatta, this dough gives you great results with minimal effort.

Prep time: 10 minutes (plus 1 hour 45 minutes resting) |
Makes: 1 batch (enough for 1 tray of focaccia, 2 medium pizzas, or 8 no-knead rolls)

325ml lukewarm water

3g instant yeast (1 tsp)

50ml olive oil

425g strong bread flour

1 tsp salt

Mix the Dough

In a large container or mixing bowl with a lid, combine the lukewarm water, yeast, olive oil, flour, and salt. Use a spatula to mix until no dry flour remains. The dough will be sticky – that's normal. Cover and rest in a warm place for 30 minutes.

Stretch and Fold

After 30 minutes, wet your hands to prevent sticking and perform a set of stretches and folds: gently pull and fold each corner of the dough into the centre. Cover and rest for another 30 minutes.

Repeat the stretch and fold step once more, then rest for another 30 minutes. The dough should now be smooth, bubbly, and airy.

Check out the Everyday & Artisan Breads chapter for recipes that build on this dough.

At this stage, the dough is ready to use in any of the following (all found later in the book):

Sea Salt & Rosemary Focaccia (p.98)

Neapolitan Style No-Knead Pizza (p.106)

No-Knead Bread Rolls (p.110)

No-Knead Ciabatta Bread (p.112)

Schiacciata Bread (p.118)

Tips for Success

Use a container with a lid to help speed up the proving and make folds easier.

Wet your hands before handling – this dough is soft and sticky.

A dough scraper or bench knife makes shaping much easier.

The dough is ready when it's soft, bubbly, and slightly jiggly when it's moved.

EMERGENCY DOUGH

This quick and simple dough is your go-to when time is short. Made with everyday ingredients and no complicated techniques, it's incredibly versatile and works as a base for rolls, flatbreads, mini baguettes, and even pizza. Fast, reliable, and beginner-friendly.

Prep time: 15 minutes (plus 1 hour resting time)

275ml lukewarm water

7g instant yeast

2 tbsp sugar

375g strong bread flour

1 tsp salt

Plain yoghurt (for brushing before baking)

Make the Dough

In a large bowl, mix the lukewarm water, instant yeast, and sugar. Add the flour and salt, then stir until a shaggy dough forms. It should look rough, sticky in places, and just starting to come together. Turn out onto a lightly floured surface and knead for 5–7 minutes, or until smooth and elastic.

Rest the Dough

Transfer to a clean bowl, cover, and let the dough rise in a warm spot for 1 hour, or until doubled in size. From here, shape and bake as needed depending on your recipe.

This dough is used in:

Pitta Bread (p.96)

Mini Baguettes (p.104)

Bagels (p.138)

Tips for Success

Instant yeast can be added straight to the flour – no activation needed.

Knead until the dough feels soft, stretchy, and smooth.

Rest the dough somewhere warm to speed up the rise. For a warm environment, preheat your oven to its lowest setting (around 30°C), then turn it off and place the dough inside to rise.

BRIOCHE DOUGH

This brioche dough is soft, buttery, and incredibly versatile. It's a base dough that works beautifully for a variety of sweet and savoury bakes, from soft buns to rich breads. With its tender texture and slight sweetness, it's perfect for creating bakery-style treats right at home. This dough also serves as the perfect foundation for various fillings, making it a go-to for all sorts of delicious bakes. For more ideas and inspiration, see the Enriched & Flavoured Breads chapter.

Prep time: 15 minutes (plus 2 hours resting time)

200ml lukewarm milk

30g unsalted butter, softened

15g caster sugar

340g strong white bread flour

5g salt

7g instant yeast

Mix the Wet Ingredients

In a bowl, combine the lukewarm milk, softened butter, and sugar. Stir to dissolve the sugar and melt the butter into the milk.

Combine the Dry Ingredients

Add the strong white bread flour, salt, and instant yeast to the wet mixture. Mix until the ingredients start to come together.

Knead the Dough

Turn the dough out onto a floured surface and knead for 8–10 minutes, or until the dough becomes smooth and elastic. The kneading step is essential to get a soft, fluffy texture in the finished buns.

Rest the Dough

Place the dough in a bowl, cover with a tea towel or cling film, and let it rise in a warm place for 1½ to 2 hours, or until doubled in size. The dough is now ready to use.

Tips for Success

Kneading the dough until smooth and elastic is key for a soft, fluffy texture.

Be patient and let the dough rise properly – it makes all the difference!

Brioche baking times will vary depending on the recipe, see the Enriched & Flavoured Breads chapter for more guidance.

SHORTCRUST PASTRY

This simple shortcrust pastry is flaky, buttery, and the perfect base for all your favourite pies and tarts. For more pastry inspiration and recipes that build on this dough, flick through to the Pâtisserie & Pastries chapter.

Prep time: 15 minutes

375g plain flour

100g caster sugar

200g cold unsalted butter, cubed

75ml milk

Make the Pastry

In a large bowl, combine the plain flour and sugar. Add the cold butter and use your fingertips to rub it into the flour until the mixture resembles breadcrumbs. Alternatively, use a food processor to speed up this step.

Bring it Together

Slowly add the milk and mix until the dough just comes together. Be careful not to overwork it – you want the dough to stay crumbly. Bring the dough together into a disc and wrap in cling film.

Chill Before Use

Once the dough is prepared, refrigerate it for at least 15 minutes before using. This helps keep the butter cold and results in a flakier texture.

Tips for Success

Always use cold butter for a flakier texture.

Don't overwork the dough – overworking makes the pastry tough.

The more you chill the dough, the flakier the result, especially before rolling out and baking.

ROUGH PUFF PASTRY

This quick and easy pastry gives you buttery, crisp layers without the long laminating process of traditional puff pastry. It's perfect for a mille-feuille, or an even easier pain au chocolat. You'll still get all the flake and lift, with just a few simple folds and plenty of cold butter.

Prep time: 30 minutes (plus 45–60 minutes chilling)

250g strong bread flour

15g caster sugar

5g salt

180g cold unsalted butter, cubed

150ml cold water or milk

Prepare the Dough

In a large bowl, whisk together the flour, sugar, and salt. Add the cold cubed butter and make a well in the centre, then pour in the cold water or milk. Stir gently until the dough just comes together – it should be shaggy and slightly sticky, with lumps of butter still visible.

Roll and Fold

Turn the dough onto a lightly floured surface and roll it into a long rectangle. Fold the dough into thirds: bring the bottom third up, then the top third down over it (like folding a letter). Rotate the dough 90°, then repeat the rolling and folding twice more for a total of three folds.

If the dough gets too soft or sticky at any point, chill it for 15–20 minutes before continuing.

Chill the Dough

Wrap the folded dough in cling film and chill for at least 30 minutes before using. This allows the gluten to relax and the butter to firm up again.

Check out the Pâtisserie & Pastries chapter for recipes that build on this dough.

This dough is used in:

Za'atar & Harissa Cheese Twists (p.158)

Easy Pain au Chocolat (p.180)

Tips for Success

Keep everything cold, especially the butter. If the butter is too warm it will melt into the dough and ruin the layers.

Don't overwork – aim for distinct butter pieces throughout.

If the dough is sticky or hard to roll, chill it.

Light flouring helps with rolling without drying out the dough.

You can freeze the dough after the final chill and use it within a month.

BAKERY-STYLE FLAKY PASTRY

Making buttery, flaky pastries from scratch is magical. Laminated dough can seem intimidating, but it's easier than you think, and this recipe breaks it down into simple steps. The reward of pulling flaky pastries from your oven is unmatched. Practice and experiment with different shapes and fillings. The possibilities are endless!

Prep time: 1 hour (plus 4 hours, or overnight, chilling and 1–2 hours proving)
| Bake time: 20–25 minutes | Makes: 8–10 pastries

100ml lukewarm water

7g instant yeast

1 medium egg (plus extra for the egg wash)

250g strong white bread flour

30g caster sugar

5g salt

10g skimmed milk powder

30g unsalted butter, softened

180g cold unsalted butter, for laminating

Prepare the Dough

In a large mixing bowl, combine the water, yeast, and egg. Add the flour, sugar, salt, and milk powder, then mix until just combined. Add the softened butter and knead the dough until smooth (about 5–7 minutes). Cover the bowl and let the dough rest in a warm place for 30 minutes.

Chill the Dough and Butter

After resting, shape the dough into a rectangle, wrap it in cling film, and refrigerate for 30 minutes. Meanwhile, prepare the laminating butter by placing the cold butter between two sheets of baking paper. Roll it into a 15 x 20cm rectangle, then chill for 15 minutes.

Laminate the Dough

Roll the dough out to twice the size of the butter rectangle. Place the butter in the centre of the dough and fold the edges over it like an envelope, sealing it completely.

First Fold

Roll the dough out into a long rectangle and fold it into thirds, like folding a letter. Wrap it in cling film and refrigerate for 30 minutes.

Second and Third Folds

Repeat the rolling and folding process two more times, chilling the dough again for 30 minutes between the second and third fold. After the third fold, wrap the dough tightly and refrigerate for at least 2–3 hours or overnight.

Shape and Fill

Roll the chilled dough into a large rectangle (about 5mm thick). Cut and shape as desired. Cover loosely and let the pastries prove for 1–2 hours, or until puffy.

For more shaping ideas and advanced fillings, check out the Pâtisserie & Pastries chapter for inspiration and new ways to use this dough.

Tips for Success

Cold dough and butter = perfect flaky layers. If the butter begins to melt, chill everything for 15 minutes.

Don't skip the folding, chilling, and proving – they're what give these pastries that bakery-quality texture.

Bake

Preheat the oven to 180°C fan. Brush the pastries with an egg wash and bake for 20–25 minutes, or until golden and flaky. Cool slightly before serving.

BASE CAKE BATTER

This simple cake batter is the foundation for everything from light sponges to rich layered cakes. Once you've mastered it, you'll have the confidence to create your favourite cakes every time. This batter is also the starting point for many bakes in the Cakes chapter, so once you've got the technique down, you can tweak it to suit any cake you're in the mood for.

Prep time: 15 minutes | Bake time: 20–25 minutes | Makes: 2 x 7-inch cake layers

3 medium eggs

175g butter, softened

175g caster sugar

1 tsp vanilla extract

175g plain flour

1 tsp baking powder

20ml milk

Weigh the Eggs

The key to a perfectly balanced cake is to use the equal weights method. Start by weighing the eggs – this ensures you get the right amount of butter, sugar, and flour. For this recipe, if your eggs weigh 175g, use the same amount of butter, sugar, and flour. This method guarantees consistency every time.

Prepare the Batter

Once you've weighed your eggs, cream the butter and sugar together until light and fluffy (about 5 minutes). This process is essential for a soft, airy texture. Add the vanilla extract, then add the eggs one at a time, mixing well after each addition to avoid curdling. Once the eggs are fully incorporated, sift the flour and baking powder and fold them into the wet ingredients gently. If the batter feels a bit too thick, add a touch of milk to loosen it up.

Bake

Preheat the oven to 160°C fan and divide the batter evenly between two lined 7-inch cake tins. For the most even layers, I recommend weighing the batter and splitting it precisely between the tins. Bake for 20–25 minutes or until a skewer inserted into the centre comes out clean. The cake should spring back when lightly touched.

Tips for Success

Always line the bottom of your cake tins with baking paper to avoid any sticky situations.

Wrap warm cake layers in cling film and place them in a ziplock bag to freeze. It keeps the cake soft, making it easier to work with later and perfect for prepping ahead!

Foundations

BASE GENOISE SPONGE

This is one of the first sponge recipes I learned, and is still one I come back to. It's so light, soft, and gets its rise from whisked eggs rather than baking powder (though I add a touch here to make it a bit more forgiving). This smaller batch is perfect for trying your first layer cake or a small Swiss roll. Once you've nailed it, you can have fun adding different flavours and fillings. See the Cakes chapter for more inspiration.

Prep time: 15 minutes | Bake time: 20–25 minutes | Makes: 1 x 6- or 7-inch round cake

2 large eggs

90g caster sugar

1 tsp vanilla extract

90g plain flour

1 tsp baking powder

Prep Everything First

Genoise relies on timing, so have your ingredients weighed and your tin lined before you start (this batter quantity works for a 6- or 7-inch cake tin).

Make the Sponge

Whisk the eggs, sugar and vanilla in a large bowl using an electric whisk or stand mixer. Beat for 6–8 minutes until the mixture is pale, thick, and holds a ribbon trail when lifted.

Add the Dry Ingredients

Sift the flour and baking powder in three parts over the mixture, folding gently after each addition. Take your time here and fold just until no flour is visible – try not to deflate the batter.

Bake

Pour the batter into your lined cake tin and smooth the top. Bake at 160°C fan for around 20–25 minutes, or until golden and springy.

Cooling

Cool in the tin for 5 minutes, then turn out onto a wire rack. Once cooled completely, carefully slice in half horizontally to create two layers.

Tips for Success

Use room-temperature eggs; they whip up better and hold more air.

Beat the eggs and sugar until light, fluffy, and when you lift the whisk, it leaves a visible trail on the surface that slowly disappears. This is called the ribbon stage and it's key to getting the rise.

Fold gently using a spatula – stirring too hard will knock out the air.

BASE COOKIE DOUGH

Think of this as your go-to, mix-and-match cookie dough. The texture is soft and chewy, with just enough
crispness around the edges. Once you've mastered this dough, you can add your own mix-ins and have fun with it.
It's the perfect starting point for building your dream cookie – and many of the recipes in the Biscuits & Cookies
chapter begin right here.

Prep time: 10 minutes (plus 15 minutes chilling) | Bake time: 12–13 minutes | Makes: 12 cookies

225g plain flour

2 tbsp cornflour

½ tsp bicarbonate of soda

½ tsp salt

150g unsalted butter, melted

175g soft light brown sugar

50g caster sugar

1 medium egg

1 tsp vanilla extract

Mix the Dry Ingredients

In a bowl, whisk together the flour, cornflour, bicarbonate of soda, and salt.

Combine the Wet Ingredients

In a separate bowl, mix the melted butter with the sugars until smooth. Add the egg
and vanilla, and whisk until combined.

Bring it Together

Fold the dry ingredients into the wet mixture until just combined – you should have
a soft dough. At this stage, fold in any mix-ins of choice like chocolate chunks or
chopped nuts etc. Don't overmix, just enough to distribute everything evenly.

Chill and Bake

Scoop the dough into 12 portions and chill in the freezer for 15 minutes. Meanwhile,
preheat the oven to 160°C fan.

Place the chilled cookie dough on a lined baking tray, leaving space between each
one. Bake for 12–13 minutes until the edges are set but the centres are still soft.

For more flavour ideas and creative twists, check out the Biscuits & Cookies chapter
for recipes that build on this dough.

Tips for Success

Chill the dough: even 15 minutes in the freezer
helps prevent spreading and gives you thicker,
chewier cookies.

Weigh ingredients for consistent results. Small
changes (especially in flour or butter) can make a
big difference to the texture.

Bake one test cookie if using new mix-ins or sizes.
Baking just one helps you adjust size, bake time,
or spacing if needed.

SCONES

A good scone recipe is the foundation for both sweet and savoury variations. This version is light, buttery, and perfect for layering with jam and cream. Mastering this base dough will set you up for other scone recipes, like Raspberry Scones or Thyme & Cheddar Scones, found in the Enriched & Flavoured Breads chapter.

Prep time: 15 minutes | Bake time: 20 minutes | Makes: 8–10 scones

425g plain flour

2 tsp baking powder

1 tbsp caster sugar

100g cold unsalted butter, cubed

225ml whole milk (with a squeeze of lemon juice)

1 egg, beaten (for egg wash)

To Serve

Jam and clotted cream

Make the Dough

In a large bowl, whisk together the flour, baking powder, and sugar. Add the cubed cold butter and rub it into the flour with your fingertips until a sandy texture is achieved.

Bring It Together

Make a well in the centre and pour in the milk with lemon juice. Use a fork to bring the dough together before gently kneading with your hands. Don't overwork it!

Shape and Cut

Turn the dough out onto a lightly floured surface and gently flatten it with your hands or a rolling pin to about 1-inch thickness. Use a round cutter to stamp out scones, placing them on a lined baking tray. Re-roll any offcuts gently to avoid waste.

Bake

Preheat the oven to 180°C fan. Brush the tops of the scones with beaten egg and bake for 20 minutes, or until golden and well-risen.

Serve

Cool slightly, then serve with jam and clotted cream.

Tips for Success

Keep your butter and milk cold for light, flaky scones. Try grating the cold butter for even distribution.

Don't overwork the dough. A light touch keeps scones tender. Knead just enough to bring it together.

Press, don't twist. When cutting out scones, press the cutter straight down – twisting can seal the edges and prevent a good rise.

Scones are at their peak on the day they're baked, but they freeze well – just reheat in the oven for a few minutes before serving.

CAKES

Everyday cakes to showstoppers

From simple one-bowl cakes to layered and rolled creations, this chapter teaches you how to balance textures, flavours, and fillings. Techniques build progressively, making even intricate cakes feel approachable.

STRAWBERRIES & CREAM CAKE

Light, fluffy sponge and a creamy filling, topped with clouds of cream and fresh strawberries, this cake has a special place in my heart. It's the perfect dessert for any occasion, whether you're celebrating a special moment or simply enjoying a slice with friends. Who knows? It might even inspire someone you love to take up baking!

Prep time: 20 minutes (plus 30–60 minutes chilling) | Bake time: 20–25 minutes | Serves: 10

For the Cake

4 medium eggs

120g caster sugar

1 tsp vanilla extract

120g plain flour

1 tsp baking powder

For the Filling

300ml double cream

75g icing sugar

1 tsp vanilla extract

For the Topping

200g strawberries, sliced (approx.)

2 tbsp strawberry jam

Tips for Success

Whisk the eggs until thick and pale for a light, fluffy sponge.

Ensure the cream filling is cold to achieve a better structure and make it easier to spread.

To speed up the chilling process, wrap the warm cake (unsliced) in cling film and place it in the freezer; this also keeps the cake soft and makes it easier to work with when adding the cream.

Prepare the Wet Ingredients

Beat the eggs, sugar, and vanilla extract together until the mixture is thick, creamy, and light in colour. This step takes about 5 minutes and is key to achieving a fluffy, airy sponge.

Add the Dry Ingredients

Sift the flour and baking powder into the wet mixture together in three parts, folding gently after each addition to avoid deflating the batter. Pour the mixture into a lined 7- or 8-inch cake tin.

Bake

Preheat the oven to 160°C fan and bake for 20–25 minutes, or until the sponge is golden brown and a skewer inserted into the centre comes out clean. It should feel springy to the touch when ready.

Prepare the Cream

While the cake cools, whip the double cream, icing sugar and vanilla extract together until thick and creamy. Divide the cream into two equal portions: one for the filling and one for the topping. Transfer each portion into separate piping bags or covered bowls, then chill in the fridge to make the cream easier to work with when assembling the cake.

Assemble the Cake

Once the cake has cooled completely, slice it in half horizontally. Pipe or dollop the cream generously onto the bottom half, then use a spoon to spread it – no need for perfection, a little mess adds a special touch. Place the second layer of cake on top, then pipe or dollop the remaining cream and spread it over the top for a rustic finish.

Make the Topping

Mix the sliced strawberries with the strawberry jam to create a glossy coating. Arrange the coated strawberries on top of the cake for a vibrant and fresh presentation. Refrigerate until ready to serve.

BLUEBERRY & CREAM SPIRAL CAKE

A soft genoise sponge filled with blueberry compote and vanilla Chantilly cream, shaped into a spiral for a showstopping finish. This is a version of a Swiss roll – but instead of rolling the sponge into a single log, it's sliced into strips and spiralled into a round cake, revealing signature swirls with every slice.

Prep time: 30 minutes | Bake time: 10–12 minutes | Makes: 1 roll cake | Serves: 6-8

For the Sponge

3 large eggs

90g caster sugar

90g self-raising flour

For the Blueberry Compote

150g fresh or frozen blueberries

75g caster sugar

1 tsp lemon juice

For the Chantilly Cream

150ml double cream

1 tbsp icing sugar

1 tsp vanilla extract

Optional:

Fresh blueberries

Mint leaves

Icing sugar (for dusting)

Tips for Success

Let the compote cool completely before assembling to avoid melting the cream.

Slice the sponge evenly for a clean swirl and even layers.

Chill the finished cake for 20–30 minutes before slicing for the neatest results.

Make the Sponge

Preheat the oven to 160°C fan and line a Swiss roll tin (approx. 23 x 33cm) with baking paper.

In a large bowl, whisk the eggs and sugar for 6–8 minutes until thick, pale, and holding a ribbon trail when the whisk is lifted.

Sift in the flour in two parts, folding gently with a spatula until just combined.

Pour into the prepared tin, spread evenly and bake for 10–12 minutes until golden and springy to the touch.

Cool and Prep

Turn the sponge out onto a clean sheet of baking paper. Peel off the lining paper and leave to cool completely, on a flat surface.

Make the Compote

Place the blueberries, sugar and lemon juice in a small saucepan. Cook over medium heat for 5–7 minutes until thickened slightly and jammy. Let it cool fully before using.

Make the Chantilly Cream

Whisk the double cream, icing sugar and vanilla until soft peaks form. Chill until ready to assemble.

Assemble the Spiral Roll

Trim the edges of the sponge if needed. Spread a thin layer of blueberry compote followed by Chantilly cream evenly over the entire surface.

Using a sharp knife or pizza cutter, slice the sponge lengthways into 6 equal strips, about 5cm wide.

Roll the first strip into a spiral and place it standing cut side up on a serving plate. Continue wrapping the remaining strips around it to form a round, layered swirl cake.

Finish with extra cream around the outside and decorate with fresh blueberries, mint leaves or a dusting of icing sugar.

Cakes

CHOCOLATE & HAZELNUT CAKE

This is my go-to when I want something rich and chocolatey but still soft and simple to make. It's based on my base cake batter, but I've added cocoa, a little coffee for depth, and a little yoghurt to keep it moist. The whipped ganache on top makes it feel a bit fancy, and the crushed hazelnuts add the perfect crunch.

Prep time: 20 minutes | Bake time: 20–25 minutes | Makes: 1 x 7-inch cake

80g plain flour

30g cocoa powder

5g baking powder

1 tsp instant coffee

Pinch of salt

100g unsalted butter, softened

90g caster sugar

2 medium eggs

1 tsp vanilla extract

2 tbsp neutral oil (sunflower or vegetable)

2 tbsp plain yoghurt or double cream

For the Topping

50g dark chocolate

50g milk chocolate

100ml double cream

Crushed toasted hazelnuts, to garnish

Prepare the Tin

Preheat the oven to 160°C fan and line a 7-inch round cake tin with baking paper.

Make the Batter

In a bowl, sift together the flour, cocoa powder, baking powder, coffee and salt.

In a separate bowl, cream the butter and caster sugar together using an electric whisk for 3–4 minutes until light and fluffy. Beat in the eggs one at a time, mixing well between each addition. Stir in the vanilla, oil, and yoghurt or cream until smooth.

Fold the dry ingredients into the wet in two parts, mixing gently until you have a smooth, thick batter.

Bake

Spoon the batter into the prepared tin and level the surface.

Bake for 20–25 minutes until the cake has risen and feels springy to the touch. A skewer inserted into the centre should come out clean or with a few moist crumbs.

Leave to cool in the tin for 10 minutes before transferring to a wire rack to cool completely.

Make the Whipped Ganache

Chop the milk and dark chocolate and place it in a heatproof bowl. Heat the cream in a small saucepan until just steaming, then pour over the chocolate. Let it sit for 1–2 minutes, then stir until smooth. Add a pinch of salt and leave to cool at room temperature until thickened.

Once cool, whip the ganache with an electric whisk until light and fluffy.

Assemble

Spread the whipped ganache over the cooled cake and scatter with crushed hazelnuts.

Tips for Success

The coffee doesn't make the cake taste like coffee, it just brings out the chocolate flavour.

Make sure your ganache is fully cool before whipping to avoid splitting.

Lightly toast the hazelnuts for even more flavour and crunch.

CHOCOLATE CHIP BANANA BREAD

Soft, moist, and packed with chocolate chips, this banana bread is the kind you'll want to bake on repeat. Made with simple ingredients, minimal effort, and the perfect balance of sweetness.

Prep time: 15 minutes | Bake time: 45–50 minutes | Makes: 1 x 6-inch loaf

100g unsalted butter, melted

75g caster sugar

50g soft light brown sugar

2 medium eggs

1 tsp vanilla extract

1 ripe banana, mashed

60ml whole milk

1 tsp lemon juice

250g plain flour

1 tsp baking powder

½ tsp bicarbonate of soda

100g chocolate chips

1 banana, sliced in half lengthways (for topping)

1 tbsp demerara sugar (for topping)

Mix the Wet Ingredients

In a large bowl, whisk together the melted butter, caster sugar and brown sugar. Add the eggs, vanilla, and mashed banana, and stir until smooth.

Make the Buttermilk

Combine the milk and lemon juice in a small bowl. Let it sit for a minute, then stir it into the batter.

Add the Dry Ingredients

Sift in the flour, baking powder and bicarbonate of soda. Fold gently until just combined: don't overmix.

Stir in the Chocolate Chips

Fold the chocolate chips through the batter, then pour into a greased or lined loaf tin.

Add the Topping

Place the sliced banana on top, cut side up. Sprinkle with demerara sugar for a caramelised crust.

Bake

Bake at 160°C fan for 45–50 minutes, or until golden and a skewer inserted into the centre comes out clean.

Cool and Serve

Let the loaf cool completely in the tin before slicing (if you can wait).

Tips for Success

The riper the banana the better; black spots mean more flavour.

Don't overmix the batter, keeping the crumb soft and tender.

Sprinkle a few extra chocolate chips on top before baking for a gooey finish.

FRAISIER CAKE

Soft genoise sponge, vanilla crème mousseline, and fresh strawberries – this is one of those bakes that looks
like it came from a bakery window. Light, creamy and best made in strawberry season, it's a proper showstopper
that's surprisingly simple to pull together.

Prep time: 45 minutes (plus 2–3 hours chilling) | Bake time: 25 minutes | Makes: 1 x 7-inch cake | Serves: 6–8

For the Vanilla Crème Mousseline

240ml whole milk

80g caster sugar (divided into 2 parts)

1 tsp vanilla paste

3 egg yolks

2 tbsp cornflour

150g unsalted butter, softened

For the Genoise Sponge

2 large eggs

80g caster sugar

1 tsp vanilla extract

80g plain flour

1 tsp baking powder

To Assemble

250g fresh strawberries, halved

2 tbsp strawberry jam

For the Chantilly Cream

150ml double cream

50g icing sugar

1 tsp vanilla extract

Tips for Success

Acetate gives the cake clean edges and helps hold
its shape while it sets.

Don't skip the chill time, the cake needs at least
2–3 hours in the fridge to set properly before
slicing.

Make the Crème Mousseline

In a saucepan, heat the milk, 40g of the sugar, and vanilla paste until just simmering.

In a separate bowl, whisk the egg yolks and remaining 40g sugar until smooth, then
whisk in the cornflour until fully combined.

Slowly pour the hot milk into the egg mixture, whisking constantly. Return
everything to the pan and cook over medium heat, whisking until thickened.

Transfer to a bowl, cover the surface with cling film, and chill completely.

Once cool, whisk in the softened butter a little at a time until smooth and fluffy.

Make the Genoise Sponge

Preheat the oven to 160°C fan and line a deep 7-inch cake tin.

In a large bowl, whisk the eggs, sugar and vanilla together for 6–8 minutes until pale,
thick, and tripled in volume.

Sift in the flour and baking powder in three parts, folding gently after each addition.

Pour the batter into the tin and bake for 25 minutes, or until golden and springy.

Let the sponge cool completely, then slice in half horizontally.

Assemble the Cake

Use a springform tin or one with removable sides to make it easier to unmould the
cake once it's set. If you have a cake ring (adjustable ones work great), that's even
better. Line the inside edge of the tin with a strip of acetate (or baking paper if you
don't have any). Press it against the sides and tape it in place if needed – this helps the
cake hold its shape and gives you clean, smooth edges once you remove the tin.

Place one sponge layer in the base and brush with strawberry jam.

Arrange halved strawberries around the inside edge of the tin, cut side facing out.

Pipe the crème mousseline between the strawberries and spread a layer across the
sponge. Top with the second sponge and press down gently.

Chill for at least 2–3 hours to set.

Finish with Chantilly cream

Whisk the double cream, icing sugar and vanilla until stiff peaks form.

Pipe on top of the cake (you can decorate it however you like) and finish with extra
strawberries or crushed pistachios, this is optional.

Carefully remove from the tin and peel away the acetate before serving.

CINNAMON ROLL CAKE

The perfect autumn dessert! If you're craving the flavour of a cinnamon roll but don't have time to make dough, this cake is your shortcut. It's soft, warm, spiced, and so easy to throw together. I love making this during the colder months – it tastes and looks just like a cinnamon roll, but with half the effort.

Prep time: 25 minutes | Bake time: 30–35 minutes | Makes: 1 x 7-inch cake

For the Cake

225g plain flour

2 tsp baking powder

120g caster sugar

Pinch of salt

180ml milk

1 egg

1 tsp vanilla extract

60ml oil

For the Cinnamon Filling

60g butter, softened

45g soft brown sugar

½ tbsp plain flour

1 tsp ground cinnamon

For the Glaze

45g icing sugar

60g cream cheese

¼ tsp vanilla extract

1 tbsp milk

Make the Filling

Mix together the softened butter, brown sugar, flour, and cinnamon until smooth. Transfer to a piping bag and set aside.

Make the Batter

In a bowl, combine the flour, baking powder, sugar, and salt. In a separate jug, whisk together the milk, egg, vanilla, and oil. Pour the wet ingredients into the dry and mix until smooth.

Pour the batter into a lined 7-inch cake tin.

Add the Swirl

Starting from the centre, pipe the cinnamon filling in a spiral pattern over the top of the batter, working your way out to the edge. This creates the classic cinnamon roll swirl once baked.

Bake

Preheat the oven to 160°C fan. Bake for 30–35 minutes, or until golden and a skewer comes out clean.

Glaze

While the cake is still warm, mix together all glaze ingredients and pour over the top. Let it settle into the warm cake before serving.

Tips for Success

Pipe the swirl gently on top; pressing too hard can cause the filling to sink and disappear into the batter.

Mix the batter just until smooth as overmixing can make the cake tough instead of light and fluffy.

Glaze while warm so it melts into the top and creates that gooey, cinnamon roll-like finish.

LEMON POPPY SEED CREAM LOAF

This is like something you'd find in a bakery. It takes a regular lemon loaf and turns it into something a little more special with a whipped lemon cream, and a spoonful of lemon curd on top. Simple to make, but with a few extra touches that make it feel worth the effort.

Prep time: 40 minutes | Bake time: 35–40 minutes | Makes: 6–8 slices

For the Loaf

Zest of 1 lemon

1 tsp lemon extract

150g caster sugar

4 medium eggs

70g unsalted butter, melted

60ml warm milk

200g plain flour

1 tsp baking powder

2 tbsp poppy seeds

For the Lemon Curd

2 egg yolks

50g caster sugar

30ml lemon juice

Zest of ½ lemon

40g unsalted butter

For the Lemon Cream

250ml double cream

50g icing sugar

½ tsp lemon extract

To Finish

Caster sugar, for coating slices

Edible flowers (optional)

Tips for Success

Don't skip the lemon sugar step, it's simple but makes all the difference.

Chill the curd before assembling so it holds its shape on the cream.

Infuse the Sugar

In a bowl, rub the lemon zest and lemon extract into the caster sugar with your fingertips until the sugar is fragrant and slightly yellow. This helps release the oils from the zest and boosts the citrus flavour.

Make the Batter

Whisk the eggs and lemon sugar together until pale and airy. Add the melted butter and warm milk, and whisk to combine.

Sift in the flour and baking powder, then fold through the poppy seeds.

Bake

Pour the batter into a greased and lined loaf tin.

Use a toothpick or knife to lightly score a line down the centre, this helps control the rise.

Bake at 160°C fan for 35–40 minutes, or until golden and a skewer inserted into the centre comes out clean. Cool completely in the tin.

Make the Lemon Curd

In a heatproof bowl, whisk the egg yolks and sugar until smooth. Add the lemon juice and zest, then place the bowl over a saucepan of simmering water. Stir for 5–7 minutes until thickened. Remove from the heat and whisk in the butter until smooth. Let it cool before using.

Make the Lemon Cream

Whisk the double cream, icing sugar and lemon extract until soft peaks form. Chill until ready to assemble.

Finish and Assemble

Once the loaf is cool, slice it into 6–8 thick slices. Dip the cut sides of each slice in caster sugar to coat.

Lay the slices flat and spoon or pipe a dollop of cream on top of each slice.

Using the back of a spoon, gently press and drag to create a small well. Fill with a spoonful of lemon curd.

Decorate with edible flowers, if using.

RASPBERRY & CHANTILLY CREAM SWISS ROLL

A light and elegant Swiss roll made with my base genoise recipe. Filled with a homemade vanilla Chantilly cream and raspberry jam, this is a simple yet impressive bake!

Prep time: 25 minutes (plus 30 minutes chilling time) | Bake time: 10–12 minutes
| Makes: 1 Swiss roll | Serves: 6–8

For the Sponge

2 large eggs

90g caster sugar

90g self-raising flour

For the Raspberry Jam

150g fresh or frozen raspberries

75g caster sugar

1 tsp lemon juice

For the Chantilly Cream

150ml double cream

1 tbsp icing sugar

1 tsp vanilla extract

To Serve

Fresh raspberries

Icing sugar (for dusting)

Tips for Success

Roll the sponge while it's still warm, this sets the shape and prevents cracking.

Don't overfill or the roll may split when you assemble it.

Let the jam cool completely before spreading, or it will melt the cream.

Make the Sponge

Preheat the oven to 160°C fan and line a Swiss roll tin (approx. 23 x 33cm) with baking paper.

In a large bowl, whisk the eggs and sugar together for 6–8 minutes using an electric hand whisk or stand mixer, until the mixture holds a ribbon trail when lifted.

Sift in the flour in two batches, folding gently after each addition. Be careful not to knock out the air.

Pour the batter into the lined tin and use a spatula to spread it evenly to the edges.

Bake for 10–12 minutes until golden and just springy to the touch – don't overbake or it may crack when rolled.

Roll the Sponge

While the sponge is still warm, turn it out onto a clean sheet of baking paper. Peel off the lining paper, then roll the sponge up from the short edge using the paper to help. Leave to cool completely, rolled up, in the fridge.

Make the Jam

In a small saucepan, combine the raspberries, sugar and lemon juice. Cook over medium heat for 5–7 minutes until the fruit breaks down and the mixture thickens slightly. Let it cool fully before using.

Make the Chantilly cream

In a mixing bowl, whisk the double cream, icing sugar and vanilla until soft peaks form. Chill until ready to use.

Assemble

Carefully unroll the cooled sponge. Spread a thin layer of raspberry jam followed by a layer of Chantilly cream. Gently roll the sponge back up.

If desired, spread more cream over the outside and decorate with fresh raspberries or a dusting of icing sugar.

MAISAM'S CARROT CAKE

A light and airy take on the classic carrot cake. This version is soft, spiced, and simple to make, with grated carrot and crushed walnuts folded into a delicate sponge. Topped with a smooth cream cheese frosting, it's a go-to for spring bakes or any time you want something gently sweet and satisfying.

Prep time: 20 minutes | Bake time: 25–30 minutes | Makes: 1 x 7-inch cake | Serves: 6–8

3 medium eggs

120g soft light brown sugar

1 tsp vanilla extract

1 tsp ground cinnamon

40ml neutral oil (sunflower or vegetable)

120g self-raising flour

½ tsp baking powder

40g crushed walnuts

100g finely grated carrots

For the Cream Cheese Frosting

150ml double cream

100g full-fat cream cheese

75g icing sugar

1 tsp vanilla extract

To Assemble

Pistachios, crushed

Prepare the Tin

Preheat the oven to 160°C fan and line a 7-inch round cake tin with baking paper.

Make the Cake

In a mixing bowl, whisk together the eggs, brown sugar, vanilla and cinnamon using an electric hand whisk until the mixture is pale and has doubled in volume.

With the mixer running on low, slowly pour in the oil in a steady stream until fully combined.

Sift in the flour and baking powder in two parts, folding gently to avoid knocking out the air. Add a teaspoon of flour to the crushed walnuts and toss (this helps stop them sinking).

Add the floured walnuts and grated carrots to the batter and fold through until just combined.

Bake

Pour the batter into the prepared tin and bake for 25–30 minutes until golden and risen. A skewer inserted into the centre should come out clean.

Leave to cool completely in the tin.

Make the Frosting

In a bowl, whisk the double cream, cream cheese, icing sugar and vanilla together until thick and smooth.

Assemble

Once the cake is completely cool, spread or pipe the cream cheese frosting over the top or fill and frost and sprinkle with crushed pistachios. The choice is completely yours!

Tips for Success

Whipping the eggs and sugar properly gives this cake its signature lightness, so don't skip this step.

Use finely grated carrot so it blends seamlessly into the sponge.

Chill the frosting for 10–15 minutes if it feels too soft to spread.

ORANGE MADELEINES

These soft, golden sponge cakes are light, buttery, and gently scented with citrus. Madeleines are a French classic, and this simplified version is ideal for beginner bakers. Chill the batter before baking for that perfect domed rise.

Prep time: 15 minutes (plus 40 minutes chilling) | Bake time: 12–15 minutes | Makes: 12 madeleines

2 eggs

120g caster sugar

Zest of 1 orange

1 tsp vanilla paste

120g plain flour

½ tsp baking powder

100g unsalted butter, melted and slightly cooled

Prepare the Batter

In a large bowl, whisk together the eggs, sugar, orange zest, and vanilla paste until pale and fluffy.

Add the Dry Ingredients

Sift the flour and baking powder into the mixture in two stages, folding gently after each addition until just combined.

Incorporate the Butter

Pour in the melted butter and fold it through until the batter is smooth and glossy.

Chill the Batter

Cover and chill the batter in the fridge for 40 minutes. This helps the madeleines rise into their classic domed shape.

Bake the Madeleines

Preheat the oven to 190°C fan. Lightly grease a madeleine tin with butter and a dusting of flour. Spoon or pipe the chilled batter into the moulds, filling each about ¾ full. Bake for 8–10 minutes, or until golden and puffed.

Cool and Serve

Remove the madeleines from the tin and transfer to a wire rack to cool. Dust with icing sugar, if you like, and serve fresh.

Tips for Success

Chill the batter to help create a domed shape.

Lightly grease the tin with some butter and a dusting of flour.

Don't overfill the moulds; ¾ full gives the best rise.

Best eaten fresh but can be frozen and gently reheated in the microwave for a few seconds.

Try dipping the ends in melted chocolate!

Cakes

RASPBERRY & WHITE CHOCOLATE BROWNIES

Rich, fudgy brownies with bursts of tart raspberries and creamy white chocolate. This is the kind of bake that disappears when shared with family and friends. Perfect for when you want something indulgent but simple to make.

Prep time: 15 minutes | Bake time: 20–25 minutes | Makes: 8–10 brownies

200g dark chocolate

100g unsalted butter

4 tbsp cocoa powder

3 eggs

150g caster sugar

100g brown sugar

1 tsp vanilla extract

80g plain flour

80g white chocolate, chopped

100g fresh or frozen raspberries

Melt the Chocolate

In a heatproof bowl, gently melt the dark chocolate, butter and cocoa powder over a pan of simmering water, stirring until smooth. Set aside to cool slightly.

Whisk the Eggs and Sugar

In a separate bowl, whisk the eggs, caster sugar, brown sugar and vanilla together for 4–5 minutes until pale and fluffy.

Combine

Pour the cooled chocolate mixture into the egg mixture and fold gently until just combined.

Fold in the Flour

Sift in the flour and fold through carefully, being careful not to overmix.

Assemble and Bake

Pour the batter into a lined 8-inch square tin. Scatter over the chopped white chocolate and raspberries.

Bake at 160°C fan for 20–25 minutes until the edges are set but the centre is still slightly soft.

Cool and Slice

Leave the brownies to cool completely in the tin for 1–2 hours before slicing. This helps them set and gives the best fudgy texture.

Tips for Success

Don't overbake the brownies, look for a slight wobble in the centre when you take them out.

For extra fudginess, chill in the fridge for a few hours before slicing.

If using frozen raspberries, add them straight from the freezer so they don't bleed too much.

Cakes

PISTACHIO & CHOCOLATE MARBLE BUNDT CAKE

A beautifully marbled Bundt cake combining the nutty richness of pistachios with the indulgence of chocolate. This cake is moist, visually stunning, and topped with a luscious chocolate ganache, pistachio cream and a sprinkle of crushed pistachios for the perfect finish. It's as elegant as it is delicious, and it's ideal for special occasions or simply an afternoon treat.

Prep time: 20 minutes | Bake time: 35–40 minutes | Serves: 10–12

For the Cake

180g unsalted butter, softened (plus extra, melted, to grease)

180g caster sugar

3 medium eggs

1 tsp vanilla extract

180g plain flour

5g baking powder

35ml whole milk

3 tbsp cocoa powder

50g pistachios, crushed

For the Topping

50ml double cream

50g milk chocolate, chopped

Pistachio cream, melted (optional)

Pistachios, crushed

Tips for Success

Use a pastry brush to coat your Bundt tin thoroughly with melted butter, then dust with flour for an easy release.

Be careful not to overmix the batter once you've added the flour; gently fold in the dry ingredients to keep the cake light and tender.

Make the Batter

Cream the butter and caster sugar together for about 5 minutes until light and fluffy. Add the eggs one at a time, mixing well after each addition, then stir in the vanilla extract.

Add the Dry Ingredients

Sift in the flour and baking powder, then fold into the wet mixture. Add the milk and mix until the batter is smooth.

Prepare the Tin

Divide the batter evenly between two bowls. Stir the cocoa powder into one bowl and the crushed pistachios into the other. Brush a Bundt tin generously with melted butter, ensuring all the crevices are covered. Dust lightly with flour to prevent sticking.

Layer and Marble

Spoon alternate layers of the chocolate and pistachio batters into the prepared tin. Use a skewer or the handle of a teaspoon to swirl the batters together gently, creating a marbled effect.

Bake

Preheat the oven to 160°C fan. Bake the cake for 35–40 minutes or until a skewer inserted into the centre comes out clean. Let the cake cool in the tin for 10 minutes, then carefully turn it out onto a wire rack to cool completely.

Prepare the Ganache

Warm the double cream in a saucepan over a low-medium heat. When it begins to simmer, remove it from the heat and add the milk chocolate. Stir until smooth and glossy, then set aside to cool slightly before using.

Decorate and Serve

Drizzle the cake with melted pistachio cream, if using, and chocolate ganache. Sprinkle crushed pistachios over the top for a final flourish. Dust with icing sugar before serving, if desired.

Cakes

BERRY CRUMBLE CAKE

There's something about a buttery cake packed with berries and topped with a crunchy crumble that just feels like summer. This one's soft, simple, and the kind of cake you can snack on all day – no occasion needed. Fresh or frozen berries both work, so you can make it whenever the craving hits.

Prep time: 20 minutes | Bake time: 30 minutes | Makes: 8–10 slices

For the Crumble Topping

50g cold unsalted butter, cubed

100g plain flour

30g caster sugar

For the Cake

160g unsalted butter, softened

160g caster sugar

3 medium eggs

1 tsp vanilla extract

160g plain flour

5g baking powder

30ml milk

250g mixed berries, fresh or frozen

Make the Crumble

In a bowl, rub the cold butter into the flour and sugar using your fingertips until it resembles coarse breadcrumbs. Set aside.

Make the Cake Batter

In a separate bowl, cream the softened butter and caster sugar together for 4–5 minutes until light and fluffy.

Beat in the eggs one at a time, mixing well after each addition. Stir in the vanilla extract.

Sift in the flour and baking powder, then fold gently until just combined. Add the milk and mix until smooth.

Assemble the Cake

Pour the batter into a lined 8-inch cake tin and smooth the top. Scatter the berries over the surface, then sprinkle over the crumble topping.

Bake

Bake at 160°C fan for 30 minutes, or until golden and a skewer inserted into the centre comes out clean.

Cool and Serve

Leave the cake to cool in the tin for 10 minutes before transferring to a wire rack. Best served slightly warm.

Tips for Success

If using frozen berries, add them straight from the freezer – no need to defrost.

Don't overmix the crumble or it'll lose its texture.

This cake keeps well for a few days in an airtight container, but let's be real – it rarely lasts that long!

Cakes

TIRAMISU CAKE

I made this for my mum's birthday, and it's become one of my favourites ever since. It's light but rich, creamy but not too sweet and if you love tiramisu, you'll definitely love this. It uses my base genoise sponge (from the Foundations chapter), brushed with coffee and layered with a whipped mascarpone cream, then finished with a dusting of cocoa.

Prep time: 25 minutes | Bake time: 25 minutes | Makes: 1 x 7-inch cake

2 large eggs

90g caster sugar

1 tsp vanilla extract

90g plain flour

1 tsp baking powder

For the Whipped Mascarpone Cream

150ml double cream

75g mascarpone cheese

60g icing sugar

½ tsp vanilla paste or extract

To Finish

40ml freshly brewed coffee, for brushing

Cocoa powder, for dusting

Prepare the Tin

Preheat the oven to 160°C fan and line a deep 7-inch cake tin with baking paper.

Make the Sponge

In a large bowl, whisk the eggs, sugar, and vanilla together for 6–8 minutes until thick, pale, and holding a ribbon trail.

Sift in the flour and baking powder in three parts, folding gently after each addition until no flour remains.

Pour into the prepared tin and bake for 25 minutes until golden and springy. Leave to cool completely.

Make the Cream

Place the double cream, mascarpone, icing sugar and vanilla in a bowl.

Whip everything together using an electric whisk until smooth, thick, and creamy. Transfer to a piping bag and chill until needed.

Assemble

Once the sponge is cool, slice it in half horizontally to create two layers.

Brush the first layer with coffee, then pipe a layer of the cream and dust lightly with cocoa powder.

Top with the second sponge layer, then cover the whole cake with more of the cream. Finish with a final dusting of cocoa powder.

Tips for Success

Whip the eggs and sugar really well for a light sponge, don't skip the ribbon stage.

Chill the cream slightly before piping to help it hold its shape.

Use just enough coffee to soak the sponge. 1–2 tbsp is enough to soak in without making it soggy.

APRICOT & STRAWBERRY CAKE

A soft, buttery sponge topped with juicy apricots and strawberries. This cake is simple to make and works beautifully with other fruits too – try it with peaches, raspberries or whatever's in season. Perfect for a light summer dessert or an easy afternoon bake.

Prep time: 15 minutes | Bake time: 30 minutes | Makes: 1 x 7-inch cake

160g unsalted butter, softened

160g caster sugar

3 medium eggs

1 tsp vanilla extract

160g plain flour

5g baking powder

3–4 fresh apricots, sliced

4–5 strawberries, sliced

Crushed pistachios (optional)

Icing sugar, to finish

Prepare the Tin

Preheat the oven to 160°C fan and line a 7-inch round cake tin with baking paper.

Make the Batter

In a large bowl, cream the softened butter and caster sugar together using an electric hand whisk for 4–5 minutes until light and fluffy. Beat in the eggs one at a time, mixing well between each addition, then stir in the vanilla extract.

Sift in the flour and baking powder, then fold through with a spatula or whisk gently until just combined – you should have a smooth, soft batter.

Assemble and Bake

Spoon the batter into the prepared tin and level the surface. Arrange the sliced apricots and strawberries over the top and scatter with crushed pistachios, if using. Bake for 30 minutes, or until golden and springy to the touch. A skewer inserted into the centre should come out clean.

Finish

Leave to cool completely in the tin, then transfer to a plate and dust with icing sugar to serve.

Tips for Success

Make sure the butter is fully softened before creaming, which helps to create a light sponge.

Don't overmix once the flour is added. This helps keep the crumb soft and tender, and gives the finished sponge a light, delicate texture.

Use ripe but firm fruit so it doesn't release too much liquid as the cake bakes.

BISCUITS & COOKIES

Maisam's signature flavours

A mix of classic and creative cookies, focusing on flavour and texture. This chapter introduces key baking instincts – like chilling, shaping, and balancing chewiness vs. crispness – while keeping recipes simple and fun.

TIRAMISU COOKIES

If you love tiramisu and cookies, these are about to become your new favourite treat. Gooey, creamy, and with the perfect hint of coffee, these cookies capture the essence of tiramisu in a grab-and-go form. Simple to whip up, they're a delicious twist on a classic dessert that everyone will adore.

Prep time: 20 minutes (plus 15 minutes chilling) | Bake time: 12–14 minutes | Makes: 8–10 cookies

For the Dough

1 tbsp instant coffee powder

80g unsalted butter, melted

75g granulated sugar

75g soft light brown sugar

1 large egg

1 tsp vanilla extract

200g plain flour

¼ tsp bicarbonate of soda

Pinch of salt

For the Topping

120g mascarpone cheese

80ml double cream

50g icing sugar

1 tsp vanilla extract

Cocoa powder, for dusting

Prepare the Wet Ingredients

In a bowl, dissolve the instant coffee in the melted butter and stir until smooth. Add the sugars, egg, and vanilla extract to the butter-coffee mixture and mix well.

Add the Dry Ingredients

Sift in the flour, bicarbonate of soda, and salt, and gently fold to form a dough.

Chill the Dough

Scoop the cookie dough into portions using an ice cream scoop, scraping the scoop to ensure even-sized cookies. Place them on a tray and freeze for 10–15 minutes to help the cookies keep their shape during baking.

Bake

Preheat the oven to 160°C fan and line a baking tray with parchment paper. Place the chilled dough balls on the tray, leaving plenty of space between them to allow for spreading. Bake the cookies for 12–14 minutes, or until golden around the edges but soft in the middle. Cool completely on a wire rack.

Make the Cream Topping

While the cookies cool, mix the mascarpone, double cream, icing sugar, and vanilla extract until creamy. Use an electric hand whisk for quicker results.

Assemble the Cookies

Once cooled, pipe or spread the mascarpone cream on top of the cookies.

Finishing Touch

Dust with cocoa powder to complete the tiramisu look and flavour.

Tips for Success

The chilling step ensures the cookies bake evenly and stay chewy in the centre.

LEMON DAISY BISCUITS

Delicate, buttery, and shaped like little daisies, these biscuits are filled with lemon curd and perfect for springtime baking or gifting. The dough is soft and easy to work with, and using the best quality butter you can find really does make all the difference. A simple, sweet treat that looks just as lovely as it tastes.

Prep time: 20 minutes (plus 30 minutes chilling) | Bake time: 12–15 minutes | Makes: About 8 sandwich biscuits

For the Biscuits

150g unsalted butter, softened

80g icing sugar

20ml double cream

1 tsp vanilla extract

150g plain flour

35g cornflour

For the Lemon Curd

2 egg yolks

50g caster sugar

30ml lemon juice

Zest of ½ lemon

40g unsalted butter

Make the Biscuit Dough

In a bowl, beat the softened butter and icing sugar until pale and fluffy. Mix in the cream and vanilla. Sift in the flour and cornflour, then fold through with a spatula until a soft dough forms. Wrap in cling film and chill for 15 minutes.

Shape and Bake

Preheat the oven to 160°C fan. Roll out the dough on a floured surface and use a cookie cutter to cut out flower shapes (or any shape you like). Try to keep the shapes as even as possible, since they'll be sandwiched together later. Transfer to a lined tray and bake for 12–15 minutes, or until just turning golden at the edges. Cool completely before filling.

Make the Lemon Curd

In a heatproof bowl, whisk together the egg yolks and sugar. Add the lemon juice and zest, then set the bowl over a pan of gently simmering water. Stir in the butter and cook, stirring constantly, for 5–7 minutes until thickened. Remove from the heat and leave to cool.

Fill and Serve

Once the biscuits are cool, sandwich them with a small spoonful of lemon curd in the middle. Store in an airtight container and eat within a couple of days.

Tips for Success

Chill the dough before rolling to make it easier to cut and shape.

Don't overbake the biscuits; they should stay pale with just a golden edge.

Use the best butter you can find, it's the star of the recipe.

Let the lemon curd cool fully before filling to avoid a runny mess.

BUTTERY PIPED BISCUITS

These melt-in-the-mouth biscuits are as easy to make as they are to eat. With a soft, buttery dough and a delicate crumb, they're perfect for filling, topping, or even dipping in chocolate. The classic star-piped shape gives them that elegant, bakery-style finish.

Prep time: 20 minutes (plus 10 minutes freezing or 30 minutes chilling) | Bake time: 12–15 minutes | Makes: 15–20 biscuits

125g unsalted butter, softened

75g icing sugar

1 egg yolk

½ tsp vanilla extract

10g milk powder

135g plain flour

35g cornflour

25ml whole milk

To Top or Dip (optional)

Jam, pistachio cream, hazelnut spread, Biscoff spread, melted chocolate, nuts, etc.

Make the Dough

In a large bowl, mix the softened butter with the icing sugar until well combined and lighter in colour. Add the egg yolk, vanilla, and milk powder and mix again.

Bring It Together

Sift in the flour and cornflour, then mix to form a soft dough. Add the milk and mix until smooth.

Pipe and Chill

Transfer the dough to a piping bag fitted with a star-shaped nozzle. Pipe rosettes (or any shape you like) onto a baking tray lined with parchment paper. Freeze for 10 minutes, or chill in the fridge for 30 minutes.

Bake

Bake in a preheated oven at 160°C fan for 12–15 minutes, turning the tray halfway through. The biscuits should be pale with lightly golden edges. Cool completely before serving or dipping in chocolate, or the topping of your choice..

Tips for Success

Use softened butter for smooth piping.

Chill the piped dough before baking to help it hold its shape.

Rotate the tray halfway through baking for even colouring.

Let biscuits cool completely before dipping in chocolate or adding other toppings.

LIBYAN GHRAIBA SHORTBREAD

This is one of the most traditional Libyan bakes and one of the best. Think shortbread, but meltier and more fragrant. The secret? A good mix of ghee, almonds, and that signature cracking on top (the more, the better!).

Prep time: 20 minutes | Bake time: 18–20 minutes | Makes: 12 cookies

75ml ghee, melted

80ml sunflower oil

70g icing sugar

65g crushed almonds

½ tsp almond extract

300g plain flour

½ tsp baking powder

Whole almonds, for topping

Mix the Dough

Preheat the oven to 160°C fan and line a baking tray with parchment paper. In a large bowl, combine the ghee, sunflower oil, icing sugar, crushed almonds, and almond extract.

Bring It Together

Add the flour and baking powder and knead until the dough becomes soft, pale, and smooth – not crumbly. This step is key to achieving that classic melt-in-your-mouth texture.

Shape and Top

Roll the dough into 12 small balls and place them on the prepared tray. Press an almond into the centre of each one.

Bake

Bake on the middle shelf of the preheated oven for 18–20 minutes, or until the tops are cracked and the cookies are lightly golden at the edges. Cool completely before serving.

Tips for Success

It might seem unusual for a shortbread-style dough, but kneading until the dough becomes pale and smooth is what gives Ghraiba its signature texture.

Cracking on top is a good thing. It means the texture is just right. No cracks usually means the dough needs more kneading.

Use good quality ghee – it brings the richness and flavour that makes these cookies stand out.

PISTACHIO BROWN BUTTER COOKIES

Chewy, nutty, and filled with pistachio cream: these are the kind of cookies I daydream about. I've always had a deep love for pistachios, and this cookie recipe really lets them shine. The brown butter adds that toasty, caramel flavour, and the filling? Too good. A pinch of sea salt on top makes them completely addictive.

Prep time: 25 minutes (plus 15 minutes chilling) | Bake time: 10–13 minutes | Makes: 10–12 cookies

150g unsalted butter

150g soft light brown sugar

50g caster sugar

1 medium egg

1 tsp vanilla extract

225g plain flour

2 tbsp cornflour

½ tsp bicarbonate of soda

½ tsp salt

Green food colouring (optional)

80g crushed pistachios

75g pistachio cream, for filling

Sea salt and extra pistachios, for topping

Brown the Butter

Melt the butter in a saucepan over medium heat. Stir occasionally as it foams and starts to brown. Once it smells nutty and amber bits form at the bottom, remove from heat and pour into a large mixing bowl. Let cool slightly, then mix in both sugars until combined.

Make the Dough

Add the egg and vanilla to the brown butter mixture and stir well. In a separate bowl, whisk together the flour, cornflour, bicarbonate of soda, and salt. Add to the wet ingredients and mix until just combined. Fold in the food colouring a drop at a time to create your desired shade of green (if using) and mix in the crushed pistachios.

Shape and Fill

Scoop the dough and roll into 10 -12 balls. Press each ball flat, spoon a little pistachio cream into the centre, then pinch the edges to seal and roll back into a ball. Freeze for 15 minutes.

Bake

Preheat the oven to 160°C fan. Line a tray with parchment paper and arrange the cookies, leaving space to spread. Bake for 10–13 minutes, until the edges are set but the centres are still soft.

Finish

While warm, sprinkle with crushed pistachios and a pinch of sea salt. Cool slightly before eating.

Tips for Success

Freezing the dough helps the cookies hold their shape and keeps the filling inside.

Slight underbaking = gooey middle.

If you can't find pistachio cream, you can make a quick version by blending pistachios with a little icing sugar and cream or melted white chocolate until smooth.

SABLÉ BRETON

I first came across Sablé Breton (also known as French salted butter biscuits) while on a French baking deep dive and instantly fell in love. These golden, buttery biscuits are crumbly, easy to make and just melt in your mouth. Traditionally from Brittany and made with good quality salted butter (the key!), they're simple but feel so special.

Prep time: 15 minutes (plus 30 minutes chilling) | Bake time: 12–14 minutes | Makes: 14–16 biscuits

125g salted butter, softened

80g icing sugar

2 egg yolks (plus 1 extra for brushing)

1 tsp vanilla extract

150g plain flour

15g cornflour

½ tsp baking powder

Make the Dough

In a bowl, beat the softened butter and icing sugar together until smooth and creamy. Add the egg yolks and vanilla, then mix again until fully incorporated.

Add the Dry Ingredients

Sift in the flour, cornflour, and baking powder. Mix gently with a spatula or your hands until the dough comes together. Flatten into a disc, wrap in cling film, and chill in the fridge for 30 minutes.

Shape and Score

Roll the chilled dough to around 6–7mm thick. Use a fluted cutter (a round cutter with wavy edges) to stamp out the biscuits – this gives the biscuits a classic scalloped edge. Then place them on a lined baking tray. Lightly beat the extra egg yolk and brush it over each biscuit. Use a fork to gently score a criss-cross pattern on top.

Bake

Preheat the oven to 170°C fan. Bake the biscuits for 12–14 minutes, or until golden around the edges and set. Cool completely on the tray – they'll firm up as they cool.

Tips for Success

Use a high-quality salted butter – it's the hero of this recipe.

Chill the dough for clean edges and a smoother finish.

For extra shine, do two light coats of egg wash (let the first dry slightly before brushing the second).

These keep well in an airtight jar for up to a week... if they last that long.

 Biscuits & Cookies

CHOCOLATE HAZELNUT SABLÉ BISCUITS

Delicate chocolate sablé biscuits filled with a dreamy homemade hazelnut cream – these look fancy but are surprisingly simple to make. The biscuits have a melt-in-your-mouth texture with a light, short snap, and the creamy centre gives just the right contrast. If you've got a soft spot for chocolate and hazelnut, these are for you.

Prep time: 25 minutes (30 minutes chilling) | Bake time: 10–15 minutes | Makes: 8 sandwich biscuits

For the Biscuits

125g unsalted butter, softened

75g icing sugar

1 egg yolk

½ tsp vanilla paste

140g plain flour

35g cornflour

3 tbsp cocoa powder

For the Hazelnut Cream

75g blanched roasted hazelnuts

75g white chocolate, melted

50ml double cream

½ tsp vanilla paste

To Finish

50g dark or milk chocolate chips, melted (optional, for drizzling)

Make the Biscuit Dough

In a mixing bowl, cream the softened butter and icing sugar until light and fluffy. Add the egg yolk and vanilla and mix again until smooth.

Sift in the flour, cornflour, and cocoa powder, and fold through until a soft dough forms. Wrap and chill for 20–30 minutes.

Make the Hazelnut Cream

Blitz the hazelnuts and melted white chocolate in a food processor until smooth and creamy. Transfer to a bowl, add the cream and vanilla, and whisk until thickened. Chill until ready to use.

Shape and Bake

Preheat the oven to 160°C fan. Roll out the chilled dough on a lightly floured surface to about 5mm thickness. Cut out shapes using a cookie cutter – any shape you like, just make sure they're all similar in size so they sandwich neatly – then transfer to a lined tray. Bake for 10–15 minutes, or until set. Cool completely before filling.

Assemble

Pipe or spoon the chilled hazelnut cream onto one biscuit and sandwich with another. Drizzle melted chocolate over the top if you like.

Tips for Success

Chill the biscuits before baking to help them keep their shape.

Let the cream cool fully before assembling so it holds its shape.

TAHINI & SESAME CHOCOLATE CHUNK COOKIES

A bakery-style cookie with a twist: rich, nutty tahini meets gooey milk chocolate chunks in this chewy, soft-centred cookie. The tahini adds depth and a subtle sesame flavour that pairs so well with the sweetness of the chocolate. They come together just like my classic dough, but taste like something new.

Prep time: 15 minutes (plus 15 minutes chilling) | Bake time: 10–13 minutes | Makes: 10 cookies

150g unsalted butter, melted

150g soft light brown sugar

50g caster sugar

1 medium egg

1 tsp vanilla extract

2 tbsp tahini

225g plain flour

2 tbsp cornflour

½ tsp bicarbonate of soda

½ tsp salt

100g milk chocolate chunks

Sesame seeds, for topping

Mix the Dough

In a large bowl, pour in the melted butter. Add both sugars and whisk until combined. Mix in the egg, vanilla, and tahini until smooth.

In a separate bowl, combine the flour, cornflour, bicarbonate of soda, and salt. Fold the dry ingredients into the wet until just combined. Stir through the chocolate chunks.

Shape and Chill

Scoop the dough into 10 balls, gently press them into the sesame seeds on one side and place on a lined tray. Chill in the freezer for 15 minutes while you preheat the oven to 160°C fan.

Bake

Bake for 10–13 minutes, until golden around the edges and still soft in the middle. Let them cool on the tray for 5 minutes before transferring to a wire rack.

Tips for Success

Don't skip chilling the cookies; freezing the dough helps them bake up thick and chewy.

Press extra chocolate chunks on top before baking for a pretty finish.

RED VELVET CRINKLE COOKIES

I had my first crinkle cookie on a summer trip to Libya, where my cousin made them for me. I'd never seen anything like them: fudgy, melt-in-your-mouth, and so pretty with their crackled white tops. I knew I had to recreate my own version for this book. These red velvet crinkle cookies feel extra special and are so soft and delicious.

Prep time: 15 minutes (plus 60 minutes chilling) | Bake time: 10–12 minutes | Makes: 10 cookies

40g unsalted butter, softened

35ml sunflower oil (or any neutral oil)

120g caster sugar

1 medium egg

1 tsp vanilla extract

Red food colouring (gel preferred)

150g plain flour

20g cocoa powder

½ tsp baking powder

Pinch of salt

For the Filling

50g white chocolate bar, broken into 10 squares (for the centres)

To Coat

Granulated sugar

Icing sugar

Make the Dough

In a bowl, whisk together the butter, oil, and sugar until smooth and combined. Add the egg, vanilla, and a few drops of red food colouring, mixing until even in colour.

Sift in the flour, cocoa powder, baking powder, and salt. Fold the dry ingredients in gently until you get a thick, slightly sticky dough.

Cover and chill the dough in the fridge for 30–60 minutes until firm enough to handle.

Roll and Bake

Preheat the oven to 160°C fan and line a baking tray with parchment paper.

Scoop the dough into small balls (about 1 tablespoon each). Press a piece of white chocolate into the centre of each ball, then roll the dough around it to fully enclose the chocolate. Roll each ball first in granulated sugar, then in icing sugar, coating generously.

Place on the baking tray, spaced apart. Bake for 10–12 minutes until crackled and puffed but still soft in the middle.

Let cool slightly before transferring to a wire rack.

Tips for Success

Chilling the dough helps with shaping and creates more defined crinkles.

Rolling in both granulated and icing sugar prevents the icing sugar from being absorbed too quickly, giving a better contrast.

Don't overbake these cookies; they should feel just set around the edges but still soft in the middle.

WHITE CHOCOLATE & CORNFLAKE COOKIES

These cookies bring together that perfect mix of sweet and salty. The cornflakes add a light crunch, the white chocolate melts into the dough, and every bite lands somewhere between soft, chewy and crisp at the edges. If you've never tried cereal in cookies before, this is a good place to start!

Prep time: 15 minutes (plus 15 minutes chilling) | Bake time: 10–13 minutes | Makes: 10–12 cookies

150g salted butter, melted

150g soft light brown sugar

50g caster sugar

1 medium egg

1 tsp vanilla extract

225g plain flour

2 tbsp cornflour

½ tsp bicarbonate of soda

100g white chocolate chunks

30g cornflakes, gently crushed (not too fine)

Mix the Dough

Whisk together the melted butter and sugars until smooth. Add the egg and vanilla, then mix until well combined.

In a separate bowl, whisk the flour, cornflour, and bicarbonate of soda. Fold into the wet mixture until just combined. Stir in the white chocolate and crushed cornflakes.

Shape and Chill

Scoop the dough into balls and place on a lined tray. Freeze for 15 minutes while you preheat the oven to 160°C fan.

Bake

Bake for 10–13 minutes, or until lightly golden. The centres should still be soft. Let cool slightly before eating (they'll crisp up more as they cool).

Tips for Success

Don't crush the cornflakes too much – you want some texture.

Using salted butter adds an extra depth of flavour and helps balance the sweetness.

Biscuits & Cookies

MAISAM'S CHOCOLATE CHIP COOKIES

A deliciously simple recipe for soft, chewy chocolate chip cookies that has been my go-to for years. These cookies have been on adventures with me – they've been baked for friends at university, shared on my first day at work, and even survived two flights when I brought them to Libya for my family. They're quick to make, perfectly sweet, and always a crowd-pleaser!

Prep time: 10 minutes (plus 15 minutes chilling) | Bake time: 12–13 minutes | Makes: 12 cookies

150g unsalted butter, melted

175g soft light brown sugar

50g caster sugar

1 medium egg

1 tsp vanilla extract

225g plain flour

2 tbsp cornflour

½ tsp bicarbonate of soda

½ tsp salt

100g dark chocolate, chopped

Prepare the Wet Ingredients

In a large bowl, pour in the melted butter. Add the soft brown sugar and caster sugar and whisk until smooth. Mix in the egg and vanilla extract until fully combined.

Add the Dry Ingredients

In a medium bowl, whisk together the flour, cornflour, bicarbonate of soda, and salt. Gradually fold the dry ingredients into the wet, mixing until just combined. Stir through the chopped chocolate, ensuring it's evenly distributed.

Chill the Dough

Scoop the cookie dough into portions using an ice cream scoop and place them on a tray. Freeze for 15 minutes to help the cookies hold their shape during baking.

Bake the Cookies

Preheat the oven to 160°C fan and line a baking tray with parchment paper. Place the chilled dough balls on the tray, leaving plenty of space between them to allow for spreading. Bake for 12–13 minutes until the edges are golden but the centres remain soft.

Cool and Serve

Allow the cookies to cool on the tray for 5 minutes before transferring to a wire rack to cool completely.

Tips for Success

For a rich, balanced flavour, the use of dark chocolate is a must and my signature touch in this recipe.

Slightly underbake the cookies for gooey centres; they will firm up as they cool.

Store in an airtight container for up to 3 days or freeze the dough to bake fresh cookies later.

APPLE & WALNUT BISCUITS

These delicate, buttery biscuits are inspired by a treat I first discovered in Türkiye. They're the kind of homemade treat you're offered with a cup of tea, and they've stuck with me ever since. Buttery dough, filled with cinnamon apples and walnuts all rolled up together... so simple, but so good. They're soft, lightly crisp on the outside, and perfect for cosy autumn days.

Prep time: 30 minutes | Bake time: 15 minutes | Makes: 8 biscuits

For the Dough

100g unsalted butter, softened

30g icing sugar

1 tsp plain yoghurt

½ tsp vanilla extract

Pinch of salt

150g plain flour

For the Filling

2 small apples, peeled and grated

40g soft light brown sugar

½ tsp ground cinnamon

30g chopped walnuts

Icing sugar, to dust

Make the Dough

In a mixing bowl, cream together the butter and icing sugar until smooth. Add the yoghurt, vanilla, and salt, then mix again. Stir in the flour and bring the dough together. Cover and set aside while you make the filling.

Prepare the Filling

In a small pan, cook the grated apples with the brown sugar and cinnamon over medium-low heat for 5–7 minutes, until soft and caramelised. Stir in the walnuts and let cool.

Shape and Bake

Preheat the oven to 160°C fan. Roll the dough out into a circle about 3mm thick and divide into 8 triangles like a pizza. Place a spoonful of filling at the base of each triangle, then roll up from the base to the tip. Transfer to a lined baking tray. Bake for 15 minutes, or until lightly golden. Let cool, then dust with icing sugar.

Tips for Success

Let the filling cool fully before assembling the biscuits to keep the dough firm.

Roll the dough evenly: too thin and it'll tear when you roll; too thick and it won't crisp up properly.

These are best the day they're made, but still lovely the next day with a cup of tea.

BREADS

Everyday & artisan breads

Starting with no-knead and beginner-friendly loaves, this chapter gradually builds skills in shaping and fermentation. By the end, you will have the confidence to tackle more complex breads with ease.

PITTA BREAD

This is the kind of bread I grew up eating – warm, soft, and perfect for dipping. Made with the Emergency
Dough from the Foundations chapter, these pittas are so easy but so satisfying. All you need is a hot oven and a
bit of resting time, and they'll puff up like magic!

Prep time: 20 minutes (plus 1 hour resting and 15 minutes proving)
| Bake time: 10–12 minutes | Makes: 6–8 pittas

275ml lukewarm water

7g instant yeast

2 tbsp sugar

375g strong white bread flour

1 tsp salt

Flour, for dusting

Make the Dough

In a large bowl, mix the lukewarm water, yeast, sugar, flour, and salt until the dough
comes together. Knead for a few minutes until smooth, then cover and leave to rest in
a warm place for 1 hour, or until doubled in size.

Shape and Rest

Once risen, lightly flour your surface, divide the dough into 6–8 equal portions and
shape each one into a smooth ball, around 5mm thick. Keep them even, not too thick
or too thin, so they puff up nicely in the oven. Transfer to a lined tray, cover, and leave
to rest for 15 minutes. Preheat your oven to its highest setting (around 220°C fan or
higher) and place a tray or baking stone inside to heat up.

Bake and Serve

Carefully place the pittas onto the hot tray and bake for 10–12 minutes, or until
puffed and golden. Serve warm or let them cool and store in an airtight container.

Tips for Success

Roll evenly, not too thin or thick for the best puff.

Preheat your oven well – a high heat is the secret
to the classic pocket.

Bake directly on a hot tray or baking stone for
extra lift.

Keep covered with a clean tea towel after baking
to keep soft.

SEA SALT & ROSEMARY FOCACCIA

Focaccia is probably my favourite bread to make as it's so versatile. Golden, crisp, and packed with flavour, this sea salt and rosemary focaccia is one of the easiest breads to make. With no kneading required, the simple stretch and fold technique creates a light, airy texture. It's perfect as a side for dinner or simply enjoyed on its own with an extra drizzle of olive oil.

Prep time: 30 minutes (plus 2 hours 15 minutes proving) | Bake time: 25–30 minutes | Makes: 1 large focaccia

325ml lukewarm water

3g instant yeast (1 tsp)

380g strong white bread flour

10g salt

Olive oil, for drizzling

Fresh rosemary

Sea salt flakes

Make the Dough

In a large bowl, mix the lukewarm water, yeast, flour, and salt with a spatula until it combines to form a sticky dough. Cover the bowl and let the dough rest in a warm place for 30 minutes.

Stretch and Fold

Once it has rested, dip your hands in water to prevent sticking, then stretch one corner of the dough upwards and fold it into the centre. Repeat on all four sides. Cover and rest for another 30 minutes.

Repeat the stretch and fold once more, then leave to rest for a final 45 minutes.

Shape and Prove

Drizzle olive oil onto a baking tray and gently transfer the dough onto the tray. Stretch the dough to fill the tray, making sure not to press too hard to preserve the air and keep the focaccia light and airy.

Cover and let it rest for another 30–40 minutes until slightly puffed up.

Once proved, drizzle more olive oil on top and gently use your fingers to create dimples in the dough. Sprinkle generously with fresh rosemary and sea salt flakes.

Bake and Serve

Preheat the oven to 200°C fan. Bake for 25–30 minutes, or until golden brown and crisp on top. Allow to cool slightly before slicing.

Tips for Success

Don't skip the stretch and fold steps – they're key to that light, airy texture.

The longer the rise, the better the focaccia! You can even leave it in the fridge for up to 2 days before baking; the crumb will be incredible, and the flavour even better.

BAKERY-STYLE FOCACCIA SANDWICH

There's something about a freshly baked focaccia sandwich that feels so special. The crisp edges, soft centre, and rich olive oil flavour make it the perfect base for layering with fresh ingredients. This version uses my no-knead rosemary and sea salt focaccia and is filled with tomato, mozzarella, and pesto for a bakery-style lunch you can easily make at home.

Prep time: 10 minutes (plus 1 hour 30 minutes resting) | Makes: 4–6 sandwiches

1 batch Sea Salt & Rosemary Focaccia (p.98)
Fresh mozzarella
Sliced tomato
Green pesto

Assemble the Sandwiches

Once the focaccia is fully cooled, slice it in half horizontally, then cut into sandwich-sized portions.

Layer each with slices of mozzarella, tomato, and a generous spoonful of pesto. Serve fresh, or lightly press in a panini press for a warm, melty version.

Tips for Success

Let the focaccia cool completely before slicing to avoid squashing the crumb and flattening your sandwich.

If making ahead, layer the pesto between the tomato and mozzarella to stop the bread from getting soggy.

For extra flavour, drizzle a little olive oil inside the sandwich before serving.

This sandwich also works great with roasted vegetables or grilled chicken.

FRENCH BAKERY-STYLE BAGUETTES

These are the kind of baguettes you'd expect to find in a little French bakery – golden, crisp, and airy inside. They use the No-Knead Dough (p.16) from the Foundations chapter, so there's no kneading or complicated steps. Let the dough prove overnight in the fridge, then shape, bake, and pretend you're in Paris.

Prep time: 20 minutes (plus overnight proving) | Bake time: 20–25 minutes | Makes: 4 baguettes

325ml lukewarm water

3g instant yeast (1 tsp)

50ml olive oil

425g strong bread flour

1 tsp salt

Make the Dough

In a large bowl, mix the water, yeast, olive oil, flour, and salt using a spatula until no dry bits remain. The dough will be sticky, don't worry. Cover the bowl and place it in the fridge to prove overnight.

Shape the Baguettes

The next day, generously flour your work surface and gently tip out the dough. Dust the top with flour and divide into 4 equal pieces using a bench scraper.

Lightly shape each piece into a rough circle, then flatten slightly and roll tightly into a baguette shape. Try to keep the ends tapered if you want that classic look.

Rest and Score

Place onto a lined baking tray and let rest for 15 minutes. Then, using a sharp knife, make 2–3 shallow diagonal slits across the top of each baguette.

Bake

Preheat the oven to 200°C fan. Bake for 20–25 minutes until golden and crisp. Cool slightly before serving.

Tips for Success

A cold overnight prove helps the flavour develop and makes the dough easier to handle.

Don't skip the slashes on top – they help control how the baguettes expand in the oven.

If your dough feels too sticky to shape, add a bit more flour to your surface.

MINI BAGUETTES

These baguettes are the perfect quick bread for sandwiches – soft on the inside, golden and crisp on the outside. Made using the Emergency Dough from the Foundations chapter, they come together quickly and deliver bakery-style results without the fuss.

Prep time: 15 minutes (plus 1 hour resting and 15 minutes proving)
| Bake time: 20 minutes | Makes: 6–8 mini baguettes

275ml lukewarm water

2 tbsp sugar

7g instant yeast (2¼ tsp)

375g strong bread flour

1 tsp salt

Flour, for dusting

Plain yoghurt (for brushing before baking)

Make the Dough

In a bowl, mix the lukewarm water, sugar, and yeast. Stir to combine, then add the flour and salt. Knead until the dough is smooth and elastic. Cover and let it rest for 1 hour, or until doubled in size.

Shape and Rest

Divide the dough into 6–8 equal portions. Shape each one into a mini baguette, long and thin with slightly tapered ends. Use a little flour to stop the dough sticking as you shape. Place on a tray lined with parchment paper and rest for 10–15 minutes.

Brush, Score and Bake

Preheat the oven to 200°C fan. Brush each baguette with plain yoghurt for a rich golden crust, then score the tops with a sharp blade. Bake for 20 minutes, or until golden and crisp.

Tips for Success

Use a floured surface when shaping to avoid sticking.

The yoghurt gives the crust great colour and texture.

Score with a sharp knife or blade for that classic baguette look.

Best served fresh but great for freezing once cooled.

NEAPOLITAN STYLE NO-KNEAD PIZZA

This is one of my most popular recipes – and for good reason. The dough is soft and pillowy inside, with a golden, crisp crust. It's inspired by Neapolitan-style pizza but made easier with my no-knead method. No mixer, no fuss, just a few folds and a bit of resting time. Perfect for topping with whatever you've got, but I love keeping it classic with mozzarella, basil, and a grating of Parmesan.

Prep time: 35 minutes (plus 1 hour 30 minutes resting) | Bake time: 12–15 minutes | Makes: 3 medium pizzas

1 batch No-Knead Dough (p.16)

Plain flour, for dusting

Olive oil, for greasing

Toppings

Tomato pizza sauce

Fresh mozzarella

Grated Parmesan

Fresh basil

Prepare the Dough

Follow the No-Knead Dough method up to the final stretch and fold stage (p.16). After the last rest, generously flour your surface and use a floured bench scraper or knife to divide the dough into 3 equal portions.

Pinch and tuck each portion into a ball. Place onto a lightly oiled tray, cover, and let rest while you prepare your toppings.

Shape and Bake

Preheat your oven to 220°C fan. Working with one dough ball at a time, gently stretch or roll into a pizza base on a floured surface. Transfer to a parchment-lined baking tray. Add your toppings.

Bake each pizza for 12–15 minutes, or until the crust is puffed and golden and the cheese is bubbling.

Tips for Success

A hot oven is key – preheat it properly for best results.

Use flour on your hands and surface when shaping as it's a soft, sticky dough.

Use a bench scraper when dividing or moving the dough to avoid sticking and stretching.

Don't overload the toppings; less is more with this style.

Add fresh basil after baking so it doesn't burn.

TURKISH SIMIT

Golden, crusted in sesame, and just the right amount of chewy, simit is one of the most iconic street foods in Türkiye. You'll spot stacks of these twisted bread rings in every corner bakery and street cart across Istanbul. I had one almost every morning during my last trip, and knew I had to try making them at home. Luckily, this version is surprisingly simple and so satisfying to bake.

Prep time: 25 minutes (plus 1 hour 30 minutes proving) | Bake time: 20–22 minutes | Makes: 6 simit rings

240ml warm milk

7g instant yeast

2 tbsp honey or sugar

1 tsp salt

60ml sunflower oil

375g strong white bread flour

For Coating

30g grape molasses

90ml water

Sesame seeds, toasted

Make the Dough

In a large bowl, mix the warm milk, yeast, honey (or sugar), and salt. Add the oil and flour, and knead until smooth and elastic. Cover and leave to rise in a warm place until doubled in size (about 1 hour).

Shape and Dip

Divide the dough into 6 equal pieces. Roll each piece into a long rope (about 40cm), fold in half, then twist the two strands around each other like a two-strand plait. Bring the ends together to form a ring and pinch to seal.

In a shallow bowl, mix the molasses and water. Dip each ring into the mixture, letting the excess drip off, then press into the toasted sesame seeds to coat all over.

Rest and Bake

Place on a lined baking tray and let rest for 30 minutes. Just before baking, gently stretch each ring out into an oval.

Bake at 200°C fan for 20–22 minutes or until golden brown. Best enjoyed fresh!

Tips for Success

Toasting your sesame seeds adds extra flavour and helps them stick better. You can do this in a dry pan over medium heat, stirring until golden.

If you don't have grape molasses, pomegranate molasses or date syrup will work too.

Serve warm with cheese, olives, and tea for the full Turkish breakfast experience.

Everyday & Artisan Breads

NO-KNEAD BREAD ROLLS

This might be the easiest bread recipe I know. No folding, shaping, or kneading – just mix, rest, and bake. These rolls come out perfectly golden and crisp on the outside, with a soft, airy inside. The best part? The recipe is easily adaptable based on how many you want to make. It's low-effort, low-mess, and always reliable.

Prep time: 10 minutes (plus 1 hour 30 minutes to 2 hours resting) | Bake time: 20–25 minutes | Makes: 6–8 rolls

300ml lukewarm water

325g strong bread flour

7g instant yeast

1 tsp salt

Flour, for dusting

Make the Dough

In a bowl, mix the lukewarm water, flour, yeast, and salt with a spatula until there's no dry flour left. The dough will be sticky; don't worry, that's exactly what you want. Cover and rest in a warm place for 1 hour 30 minutes to 2 hours, or until doubled in size and bubbly.

Scoop and Bake

Preheat the oven to 200°C fan. Line a baking tray with parchment paper.

Using two spoons, scoop mounds of dough directly onto the tray – no shaping needed. Leave a little space between each one so they don't stick together as they rise.

Dust the tops with flour for a rustic finish and to help them crisp up.

Bake for 20–25 minutes, or until golden and crisp. Let cool slightly before serving.

Tips for Success

The dough is sticky, so use spoons or a dough scoop to keep it mess-free.

Don't skip the flour on top, it helps form that beautiful crust.

Best enjoyed fresh, but they freeze and reheat really well.

NO-KNEAD CIABATTA BREAD

This no-knead ciabatta recipe is perfect for beginners and seasoned bakers alike. Its simplicity and foolproof method have made it a favourite, helping countless people discover the joy of baking bread at home. With its light, airy texture and signature rustic crust, this bread is endlessly rewarding to make.

Prep time: 15 minutes (plus 1 hour 45 minutes resting and proving) | Bake time: 20–25 minutes | Makes: 2 large or 8 small ciabatta loaves

325ml lukewarm water

3g instant yeast (1 tsp)

50ml olive oil

425g strong white bread flour

10g salt

Mix the Dough

In a container with a lid, combine the lukewarm water and yeast. Stir in the olive oil, bread flour, and salt. Mix with a spatula until a sticky dough forms.

First Rest

Cover the container and leave the dough to rest in a warm place for 30 minutes.

Stretch and Fold

After the first rest, wet your hands to prevent sticking, then stretch and fold each corner of the dough toward the centre. Cover and rest for another 30 minutes.

Repeat the stretch-and-fold process, then let the dough rest for another 30 minutes.

Shape

Generously flour the work surface. Use a floured bench scraper or knife to cut the dough into rough rectangular shapes. Handle gently to preserve the air bubbles.

Final Rest

Transfer the dough rectangles to a baking tray lined with parchment paper. Let them rest for 15 minutes.

Bake

Preheat the oven to 200°C fan. Bake for 20–25 minutes, or until golden brown and crisp. Allow the loaves to cool slightly before slicing.

Tips for Success

Don't add more flour than the recipe calls for – the dough should be quite sticky as this helps create the airy crumb. You can use a spatula to mix the dough more easily.

Shape the dough carefully to maintain the air bubbles.

Use plenty of flour on surfaces and tools to prevent sticking while handing the dough.

CIABATTA TUNA, OLIVE & HARISSA SANDWICH

This one takes me straight back to childhood, it's a Libyan classic, and probably the sandwich I've eaten the most in my life. Fresh ciabatta spread with harissa, topped with tuna, a handful of olives, and that's it. Salty, spicy, comforting. It's one of the most popular sandwiches across North Africa for a reason – so simple but so, so good. Make it with the No-Knead Ciabatta (p.112).

Prep time: 10 minutes | Makes: 2 sandwiches

2 ciabatta rolls

2 tbsp harissa paste

1 tin tuna in oil, drained

A handful of pitted green or black olives

A drizzle of olive oil

Prepare the Bread

Slice the ciabatta rolls in half and lightly toast them if you like a bit of crunch.

Assemble the Sandwich

Spread a generous layer of harissa on the bottom half of each roll. Top with tuna, scatter over the olives, and finish with a drizzle of olive oil.

Serve

Close the sandwich and eat while the bread is still warm. Perfect on its own, or with a cold drink or a glass of tea if you're doing it the Libyan way.

Tips for Success

Use good quality harissa – it makes a big difference.

If you're not into spice, mix the harissa with a bit of mayo to mellow it out.

NO-OVEN BREAKFAST BREAD (ENGLISH MUFFINS)

One of the most popular breakfast breads – and for good reason! These soft, pillowy English muffins are cooked entirely on the hob, making them perfect if you don't have an oven (or just don't feel like turning it on). I love making these on slow mornings when I want something warm, fresh, and a little nostalgic.

Prep time: 20 minutes (plus 1 hour resting and 15–20 minutes proving)
| Bake time: 10 minutes | Makes: 10–12 muffins

275ml warm milk

7g instant yeast

40g butter, melted

1 egg

425g plain flour

1 tbsp sugar

1 tsp salt

Fine semolina, for dusting

Make the Dough

Add the warm milk, yeast, melted butter, egg, flour, sugar, and salt to a large bowl. Mix and knead until a smooth dough forms. Cover and rest in a warm place for 1 hour, or until doubled in size.

Roll and Cut

Dust your surface with fine semolina. Roll the dough out to about 2.5cm thick. Dust the top lightly with more semolina, then use a round cutter to cut out the muffins. Let them rest for 15–20 minutes while you preheat the pan.

Cook

Heat a frying pan or wide pot over medium-low heat. Cook the muffins for around 5 minutes on each side, with a lid on – this helps them rise and cook through evenly. Cool slightly before slicing or serving.

Tips for Success

Semolina gives the muffins that classic texture – don't skip it!

Keep the heat low so the muffins cook through without burning.

Use a lid to help the steam gently lift and puff the muffins.

Best eaten warm, but you can toast them the next day too.

SCHIACCIATA BREAD

When focaccia meets ciabatta... you get schiacciata. This rustic flatbread from Tuscany has the crispiness of a
good ciabatta and the rich, olive oil-soaked top of a focaccia. I make it using my No-Knead Dough from the
Foundations chapter – it's soft, bubbly, and perfect for this kind of bake. Serve it warm, tear it apart at the table,
or slice it in half and stuff it with your favourite fillings.

Prep time: 20 minutes (plus 1 hour 30 minutes resting) | Bake time: 20–25 minutes | Makes: 4 flatbreads

325ml lukewarm water

3g instant yeast (1 tsp)

425g strong white bread flour

10g salt

50ml olive oil (plus extra for drizzling)

Flour, for dusting

Make the Dough

In a large bowl, mix the lukewarm water, yeast, flour, salt, and olive oil with a spatula
until it comes together into a sticky dough. Cover and leave to rest in a warm spot for
30 minutes.

Stretch and Fold

Wet your hands to stop the dough sticking, then stretch one side of the dough
upwards and fold it into the centre. Repeat on all four sides, then cover and rest for
another 30 minutes. Repeat the stretch and fold one more time, and rest again for a
final 30 minutes.

Shape and Prove

Dust your work surface generously with flour and tip the dough onto it. Use a floured
bench scraper to divide it into four equal pieces. Gently shape each one into a rough
circle and transfer to a lined baking tray. Drizzle with olive oil and use your fingertips
to create dimples in the dough.

Bake and Serve

Preheat the oven to 200°C fan. Bake the schiacciata for 20–25 minutes, or until
golden and crisp on the outside. Serve warm or allow to cool before slicing.

Tips for Success

Flour your surface well when shaping – it's a
sticky dough.

Don't be shy with the olive oil; it's what gives that
classic focaccia-like top.

Everyday & Artisan Breads

SOFT SANDWICH LOAF

This is hands down one of my favourite loaves to bake – it's soft, fluffy, and perfect for everyday sandwiches or toast. It's also super simple and beginner-friendly, which makes it a great recipe to have on hand. I love how quickly it comes together, and how something so easy can feel so satisfying.

Prep time: 15 minutes (plus 1 hour 30 minutes resting and proving)
| Bake time: 25–30 minutes | Makes: 1 medium loaf

240ml warm milk

2 tbsp sugar

7g instant yeast

340g strong bread flour

1 tsp salt

Milk, for brushing

Make the Dough

In a bowl, mix the warm milk, sugar, and instant yeast. Add the flour and salt, then knead until the dough is smooth and elastic. Cover and leave to rise in a warm spot for about 1 hour, or until doubled in size.

Shape and Prove

Lightly flour your surface and shape the dough: roll it into a flat circle, then roll it tightly into a log. Pinch the seam to seal and tuck the ends under. Line a loaf tin with baking paper and place the dough inside. Let it rise again until doubled in size, around 30 minutes.

Bake

Preheat the oven to 180°C fan. Brush the top of the loaf with milk and score down the centre with a sharp knife. Bake for 25–30 minutes, or until golden brown and risen. Cool before slicing.

Tips for Success

Shaping into a tight log helps give the loaf structure.

Let the dough rise again in the tin for a soft, even crumb.

Brushing with milk gives a soft, golden crust.

Slice only once fully cooled to avoid squashing the loaf.

Everyday & Artisan Breads

WHOLEWHEAT SANDWICH SQUARES

Soft, fluffy, and made with a mix of wholewheat and white flour, these sandwich squares are perfect for lunchboxes or meal prep. Shaped like little slabs rather than long baguettes, they bake up golden and airy – great for slicing and filling. The dough comes together quickly and uses the Emergency Dough method from the Foundations chapter.

Prep time: 15 minutes (plus 1 hour resting and 15 minutes proving)
| Bake time: 20 minutes | Makes: 6–8 sandwich squares

275ml lukewarm water

2 tbsp sugar

7g instant yeast

275g wholewheat bread flour

100g strong white bread flour

1 tsp salt

Flour, for dusting

Water, for brushing

Mixed seeds (optional)

Make the Dough

In a large bowl, mix the lukewarm water, sugar, and yeast. Stir to combine. Add the flours and salt, then knead for 5–7 minutes, or until smooth and elastic. Cover and rest for 1 hour in a warm spot, or until doubled in size.

Shape and Rest

Lightly dust your work surface with flour. Divide the dough into 6–8 equal pieces, then shape each one into a square or rectangular slab. If using seeds, lightly brush the tops with water and dip or roll the top side into a plate of seeds. Place on a tray lined with parchment, leaving space between each piece. Rest for 15 minutes.

Score and Bake

Preheat the oven to 200°C fan. Use a sharp knife to make a shallow slash or cross on top of each square. Bake for 20 minutes, or until golden brown.

Tips for Success

Use a bench scraper to help shape the dough and create clean edges.

Brushing with water helps the seeds stick, along with pressing lightly if needed.

These freeze well once cooled – perfect for prepping ahead.

TOMATO & OLIVE FOCACCIA MUFFINS

These mini focaccias are a fun twist on the classic tray-baked version. Baked in a muffin tray, they're soft, fluffy, and packed with flavour from juicy cherry tomatoes, olives, and olive oil. It's the same no-knead dough from my Sea Salt & Rosemary Focaccia, just reshaped into individual portions – perfect for lunchboxes, snacking, or picnics.

Prep time: 30 minutes (plus 2 hours 15 minutes proving) | Bake time: 20–25 minutes | Makes: 10–12 muffins

325ml lukewarm water

3g instant yeast (1 tsp)

380g strong white bread flour

10g salt

For the Topping:

Olive oil, for greasing and drizzling

12–15 cherry tomatoes, halved

60g pitted olives

Make the Dough

In a large bowl, mix the lukewarm water, yeast, flour, and salt with a spatula until a sticky dough forms. Cover the bowl and let it rest in a warm place for 30 minutes.

Stretch and Fold

Wet your hands, then stretch one corner of the dough up and fold it into the centre. Repeat on all four sides. Cover and let it rest for another 30 minutes.

Repeat the stretch and fold once more, then leave to rest for a final 45 minutes.

Shape and Prove

Grease a muffin or cupcake tray with olive oil. Divide the dough evenly between the holes (it will be sticky – a bench scraper and wet hands help!). Cover and let rest for 30–40 minutes until puffed.

Top and Bake

Preheat the oven to 200°C fan. Drizzle olive oil over each muffin and gently press halved tomatoes and olives into the tops.

Bake for 20–25 minutes or until golden and crisp on top. Cool slightly before removing from the tin.

Tips for Success

Use plenty of olive oil to help the muffins crisp up beautifully.

Don't over-handle the dough when shaping, to keep it light and airy.

CHEDDAR & HERB SESAME BUNDT BREAD

A savoury twist on my no-knead dough that's honestly become a new favourite. The bread bakes up soft on the inside, golden on the outside, and is filled with pockets of melted cheddar and herbs. Baking it in a Bundt tin is super forgiving and makes the loaf look effortlessly impressive!

Prep time: 20 minutes (plus 1 hour proving) | Bake time: 30–35 minutes | Makes: 1 loaf

325ml lukewarm water

3g instant yeast (1 tsp)

425g strong white bread flour

10g salt

Olive oil, for greasing

Sesame seeds, for topping

Flour, for dusting

Grated cheddar cheese (around 100g or to taste)

1 tsp dried oregano

Make the Dough

In a large bowl, mix the lukewarm water, yeast, flour, and salt with a spatula until no dry flour remains. The dough will be sticky – don't worry! Cover and leave to rest in a warm place for 1 hour, or overnight in the fridge.

Shape and Fill

Lightly grease a Bundt or loaf tin with olive oil. Sprinkle the top, bottom and sides of the tin with sesame seeds – they help prevent the dough from sticking and give the bread a nice crust.

Tip the dough out onto a floured surface and gently flatten it. Sprinkle with grated cheese and dried oregano. Use a bench scraper to roll the dough into a rough log, then carefully lift it into the prepared tin.

Prove and Bake

Cover and leave to prove for about 30–40 minutes, or until doubled in size. Meanwhile, preheat the oven to 200°C fan.

Sprinkle the top with more sesame seeds and bake for 30–35 minutes, or until golden and crisp. Let it cool slightly before slicing.

Tips for Success

Be generous with the cheese – it creates those gooey, golden pockets.

A Bundt tin gives this loaf a fun shape, but any loaf tin will work.

Don't skip the final prove, this helps the bread rise properly in the oven.

Everyday & Artisan Breads

BREADS

Enriched & flavoured breads

Focusing on the incredible flavours you can work into your doughs and inspiring you to experiment with more advanced ingredients that will take your bakes to the next level.

TURKISH AÇMA BREAD

I'm so excited to share this recipe! Açma is a soft, fluffy, bagel-like Turkish bread that's buttery and utterly irresistible, found in almost every bakery across Istanbul's streets. A little slice of Istanbul inspired by my travels there, this recipe is easy to recreate at home and has been a favourite among my followers. It's approachable for all skill levels and worth every step.

Prep time: 20 minutes (plus 1 hour 30 minutes proving) | Cooking time: 20–25 minutes | Makes: 6

240ml lukewarm milk

2 tbsp honey (or sugar)

7g instant yeast

50ml sunflower oil

375g strong white bread flour

1 tsp salt

30g butter, softened

1 egg yolk, for the egg wash

Sesame seeds or nigella seeds, for the topping

Prepare the Dough

In a large mixing bowl, combine the lukewarm milk, honey, yeast, and sunflower oil. Stir to dissolve, then add the flour and salt. Knead until the dough is soft, smooth, and slightly sticky. Cover and leave to rise in a warm place until it doubles in size, about 1 hour.

Roll and Layer

Once the dough has risen, roll it into a thin rectangle. Brush the surface with softened butter to create the signature buttery layers. Fold the dough over itself neatly, then roll it out slightly to flatten the layers.

Shape

Slice the dough into six equal strips. Twist each strip gently and bring the ends together to form rings. Place the shaped açma on a baking tray lined with parchment paper.

Rest and Top

Cover the tray loosely and let the açma rest for another 30 minutes. When they've puffed up slightly, brush each one with egg yolk and sprinkle generously with sesame or nigella seeds.

Bake

Preheat the oven to 200°C fan. Bake the açma for 20–25 minutes, or until golden brown.

Serve and Enjoy

Serve the açma warm, plain, or with jam or soft cheese. They're perfect for breakfast or afternoon tea.

Tips for Success

A soft, slightly sticky dough ensures fluffy results.
Take care during the layering step – this makes
all the difference as the butter layers add richness.
To enjoy them for breakfast, prepare the dough
the night before and refrigerate the shaped açma
to bake fresh in the morning.

Enriched & Flavoured Breads

ORANGE BRIOCHE BUNS WITH ORANGE BLOSSOM MASCARPONE CREAM

Soft, fragrant, and filled with a light orange blossom mascarpone cream, these brioche buns are the perfect balance of richness and freshness. They're simple to make but feel like a fancy bakery-style treat, ideal for an afternoon tea or a special breakfast.

Prep time: 30 minutes (plus 2 hours 30 minutes resting and proving) | Bake time: 20–25 minutes | Makes: 8 buns

For the Dough

200ml lukewarm milk

30g unsalted butter, softened

2 tbsp orange blossom water

1 orange, zested

15g caster sugar

340g strong white bread flour

5g salt

7g instant yeast

Milk, for brushing on top before baking

For the Filling

200ml double cream

120g mascarpone cheese

40g icing sugar

2 tbsp orange blossom water

1 orange, zested

Make the Dough

In a bowl, mix the lukewarm milk, softened butter, orange blossom water, orange zest, and sugar.

Add the flour, salt, and yeast, and mix until combined. Knead for 8–10 minutes until smooth and elastic.

Cover and let rise in a warm place for 1½–2 hours, or until doubled in size.

Shape and Bake

Once risen, punch down the dough to release some of the air, then divide it into eight equal pieces. Roll into smooth balls and place on a lined baking tray.

Cover and let rise again for 45 minutes to 1 hour, until puffy, then brush with milk.

Preheat the oven to 160°C fan. Bake for 20–25 minutes or until golden brown. Let cool completely.

Prepare the Filling

In a bowl, whisk the double cream, mascarpone, icing sugar, orange blossom water, and orange zest until smooth and creamy.

Assemble the Buns

Slice off the top of each bun to create a small lid. Using scissors, cut a 'V' or heart shape into the lids to make them a little fancier.

Using a star nozzle (or any piping nozzle available), pipe the cream filling into the base of each bun.

Place the lid back on top and dust with icing sugar and extra orange zest before serving.

Tips for Success

Knead until the dough is smooth and elastic to develop the structure needed for a light, fluffy texture.

Give the dough enough time to rest to achieve softer brioche buns.

Let the buns cool completely before filling to prevent the cream from melting.

TURKISH PIDE BREAD (RAMAZAN PIDESI)

This is one of my absolute favourites. Ramazan Pidesi is a traditional Turkish bread baked especially during Ramadan and served at iftar and sahur. It's soft, slightly chewy, and topped with a beautiful diamond pattern and a sprinkle of sesame and nigella seeds. I used to make this every year, and it's one of those breads that looks impressive but comes together so easily.

Prep time: 20 minutes (plus 1 hour 15 minutes resting) | Bake time: 25–30 minutes | Makes: 1 large flatbread

240ml warm milk

2 tbsp honey

7g instant yeast

375g strong white bread flour

1 tsp fine salt

60ml olive oil

For the Egg Wash

1 egg yolk

1 tsp vinegar

2 tsp yoghurt

1 tbsp olive oil

To Finish

Sesame seeds

Nigella seeds

Coarse semolina or flour (for the tray)

Make the Dough

In a large bowl, mix the warm milk, honey, and yeast. Add the flour, salt, and olive oil. Knead until the dough is smooth and elastic, about 8–10 minutes by hand. Cover and let rise for 1 hour or until doubled in size.

Shape

Preheat the oven to 200°C fan. Sprinkle semolina or flour onto a lined baking tray.

Turn out the dough and gently stretch or press it into a large oval shape, about 2cm thick. Leave to rest for 15 minutes.

Using your fingertips, press a diamond pattern across the surface of the dough: start by outlining a border, then make intersecting diagonal lines inside it.

Finish and Bake

Whisk together the egg yolk, vinegar, yoghurt, and olive oil to make the egg wash. Brush it generously over the surface of the dough, then sprinkle with sesame and nigella seeds.

Bake for 25–30 minutes, or until golden and slightly puffed.

Serve

Best enjoyed warm from the oven with soft cheese, eggs, or a little olive oil and za'atar.

Tips for Success

Use a light touch when creating the pattern so the dough doesn't deflate.

Semolina gives the base a nice crunch, but flour works fine too.

Enriched & Flavoured Breads

CINNAMON ROLLS

These are my go-to when I want cinnamon rolls without committing to a 24-hour dough or three rise stages. They're soft, sweet, and full of warm cinnamon sugar. They also start with my Emergency Dough from the Foundations chapter, but with milk swapped in for water to add extra softness, and a little butter mixed into the dough for richness. I love finishing them with a cream cheese glaze and a sprinkle of toasted nuts for crunch. The ultimate comfort in bun form.

Prep time: 20 minutes (plus 1 hour 30 minutes resting | Bake time: 25 minutes | Makes: 8 rolls

275ml lukewarm whole milk

7g instant yeast

2 tbsp caster sugar

20g unsalted butter, melted

375g strong white bread flour

1 tsp fine salt

For the Filling

50g unsalted butter, softened

75g soft brown sugar

1 tbsp ground cinnamon

For the Glaze

60g cream cheese

2 tbsp milk

½ tsp vanilla extract

50g icing sugar

To Finish

Toasted pecans or flaked almonds (optional)

Make the Dough

In a large bowl, whisk together the milk, yeast, sugar, and melted butter. Add the flour and salt, then mix until a dough forms. Knead for 6–8 minutes until soft and smooth. Cover and let rise for 1 hour, or until doubled in size.

Shape and Fill

Roll the dough out into a rectangle, about 30 × 40cm. Spread with the softened butter all over. In a small bowl, mix the brown sugar and cinnamon, then sprinkle evenly on top.

Roll and Slice

Starting from the long edge, roll the dough up tightly into a log. Slice into 8 equal pieces and place in a lined or greased baking tin, spaced slightly apart.

Final Rise

Cover loosely with cling film and leave to rise for 30–40 minutes until puffed and touching.

Bake

Preheat the oven to 180°C fan. Bake the rolls for 22–25 minutes, or until golden and cooked through.

Finish

Whisk the cream cheese, milk, vanilla, and icing sugar together into a smooth glaze. Drizzle over the warm rolls and top with toasted pecans or flaked almonds, if using.

Tips for Success

Adding melted butter to the dough makes the rolls richer and more tender.

Use soft brown sugar for a gooey cinnamon swirl that melts beautifully into the dough.

Glaze while warm, for the perfect drip.

These keep well for a couple of days and reheat perfectly with a quick microwave blast.

BAGELS

These bagels are such a treat: chewy, golden, and that glossy crust from a quick boil. Honestly, I was surprised
how easy they were the first time I made them, using the same Emergency Dough from the Foundations
chapter, just shaped into rings and boiled before baking. They've become a go-to for me, whether it's breakfast,
lunch, or a snack straight off the tray.

Prep time: 25 minutes (plus 1 hour resting) | Bake time: 20–25 minutes | Makes: 8 bagels

1 batch Emergency Dough (p.18)

Water, for boiling

1 tbsp bicarbonate of soda

1 egg, beaten with a splash of milk or water

Toppings of choice (I like to use sesame seeds
and nigella seeds, poppy seeds, everything
seasoning or za'atar)

Shape the Dough

After the dough has rested and doubled in size, divide it into 8 equal portions. Lightly
flour your work surface to prevent sticking.

To shape the bagels: roll each dough ball into a flat circle, then roll it tightly into a
log. Flatten one end of the log and wrap it over the other end to form a ring, pinching
gently to seal.

Boil

Bring a large pot of water to a gentle boil – you'll need enough to submerge the bagels
comfortably – and add the bicarbonate of soda. Boil the bagels in batches for 30–40
seconds on each side, then transfer to a parchment-lined baking tray.

Bake

Preheat the oven to 200°C fan. Brush each boiled bagel with the egg wash and
sprinkle over your chosen toppings. Bake for 18–20 minutes, or until golden brown.
Cool slightly before serving.

Tips for Success

Boiling gives bagels their chewy texture and
shiny crust – don't skip it.

Don't overcrowd the pan while boiling and work
in batches of around 2 or 3 at a time.

A light egg wash gives a glossy finish and helps
toppings stick.

BULGARIAN POGACHA BREAD

One of the things I love most about bread is how every culture has its own version of a soft, pull-apart loaf meant for sharing. This one comes from Bulgaria and was introduced to me by a lovely follower. Pogacha is traditionally made for celebrations, and you can see why – it's golden, fluffy, and beautifully shaped. Optionally filled with cheese, this bread is a joy to make and even better to eat.

Prep time: 20 minutes (plus 1 hour 30 minutes resting) | Bake time: 20–25 minutes |
Makes: 1 tear-and-share round | Serves: 6–8

60ml water

60ml whole milk

40ml sunflower oil

1 medium egg (plus 1 for egg wash)

7g instant yeast

20g caster sugar

250g plain flour

½ tsp fine salt

Optional Filling

White cheese, such as feta or Bulgarian sirene

To Finish

Egg wash

Sesame seeds (for sprinkling)

Make the Dough

In a mixing bowl, whisk together the water, milk, oil, egg, yeast, and sugar. Add the flour and salt, and knead into a soft, sticky dough. Don't add more flour – the dough is meant to be soft. Cover and let rise for 1 hour, or until doubled in size.

Shape and Fill

Once risen, divide the dough into two equal parts. Roll each piece into a thin circle, about the size of your round cake tin. Place one circle on a sheet of baking paper. If using cheese, crumble a layer over the surface, then top with the second dough circle. If not using cheese, still layer both circles – this helps create a softer, fluffier texture as the layers rise and bake together.

Use a sharp knife or pizza cutter to divide the stacked dough into 8 triangles, like a pizza. Roll each triangle up from the wide edge to the point, like a croissant. Arrange the pieces in a greased or lined round cake tin, spacing them evenly.

Final Rise

Cover the tin loosely with cling film and let the shaped dough rise again for 30–40 minutes, or until puffed.

Bake

Preheat the oven to 180°C fan. Brush the risen dough with beaten egg and sprinkle sesame seeds over the top. Bake for 20–25 minutes, or until golden brown and cooked through.

Serve

Best enjoyed warm, pulled apart with your hands. It's soft, buttery, and perfect with tea or soup.

Tips for Success

Use a light touch when kneading – this dough is naturally sticky but becomes beautifully elastic after resting.

White cheese adds a salty contrast, but the bread is just as good plain.

KANELBULLAR (SWEDISH CINNAMON KNOTS)

These are what I make when I want something cinnamon-y, but a little more elegant than your classic gooey roll. Kanelbullar are twisted Swedish cinnamon buns, usually made with a lightly cardamom-scented dough, knotted into pretty shapes, and finished with pearl sugar instead of icing. They look fancy, but they're surprisingly easy to make – and delicious with a cup of tea.

Prep time: 30 minutes (plus 1 hour 40 minutes resting) | Bake time: 20–25 minutes | Makes: 8–10 knots

For the Brioche Dough Base

200ml lukewarm milk

30g unsalted butter, softened

15g caster sugar

1 tsp ground cardamom

340g strong white bread flour

5g fine salt

7g instant yeast

For the Filling

40g unsalted butter, softened

50g light brown sugar

1 tbsp ground cinnamon

To Finish

1 egg (for egg wash)

Pearl sugar (optional)

Make the Dough

In a large bowl, whisk together the lukewarm milk, softened butter, sugar, and cardamom. Add the flour, salt, and yeast, then mix until a dough forms. Knead for 8–10 minutes until smooth and elastic. Cover and let rise for 1 hour or until doubled.

Fill and Shape

Once risen, roll the dough into a rectangle about 30 × 40cm. Spread with the softened butter all over. In a small bowl, mix the brown sugar and cinnamon, then sprinkle evenly on top Fold the dough rectangle in half to cover the filling, like closing a book.

Use a sharp knife or pizza cutter to slice the dough into strips about 2cm wide. Twist each strip, then knot it loosely and tuck the ends underneath. Place on a lined tray.

Final Rise

Cover loosely with cling film and let rise for 30–40 minutes, until puffed.

Bake

Preheat the oven to 180°C fan. Brush the buns with egg wash and sprinkle generously with pearl sugar. Bake for 20–25 minutes or until golden brown.

Serve

Best enjoyed slightly warm – they're fluffiest fresh from the oven, still warm with a little crunch on top.

Tips for Success

Don't skip the cardamom in the dough – it's what makes these kanelbullar, not just fancy cinnamon rolls.

The knot shape looks impressive but is very forgiving – rustic is good.

SOFT DINNER ROLLS

These are the kind of rolls you make once and then never stop making. They're soft, pillowy, and come together
so easily using my Emergency Dough from the Foundations chapter: just swap the water for milk and you've
got the perfect side for soups, or just a warm snack spread with butter. I like brushing them with melted butter
(sometimes garlic butter) straight from the oven for a little extra shine and flavour.

Prep time: 20 minutes (plus 1 hour 40 minutes resting) | Bake time: 25–30 minutes | Makes: 8 rolls

275ml lukewarm whole milk

7g instant yeast

2 tbsp caster sugar

1 tsp fine salt

375g strong white bread flour

To Finish

2 tbsp melted salted butter (plain or garlic)

Make the Dough

In a large bowl, whisk together the warm milk, yeast, and sugar. Add the flour and salt
and knead until the dough is smooth and springy, around 10–12 minutes by hand or
8 minutes in a mixer. Cover and let rise for 1 hour, or until doubled in size.

Shape

Turn the dough out onto a lightly floured surface. Divide into 8 equal pieces and
shape each one into a smooth ball. Arrange them in a lined or buttered square tin or
baking dish, spaced just slightly apart so they'll rise into each other as they bake.

Final Rise

Cover loosely and let rise for 30–40 minutes until puffed and just touching.

Bake

Preheat the oven to 200°C fan. Bake for 25–30 minutes, or until golden on top and
hollow-sounding when tapped on the bottom.

Finish

While still warm, brush the tops generously with melted butter (or garlic butter if
you're going savoury). Let cool slightly, then serve.

Tips for Success

Swapping water for milk makes the crumb extra
soft and fluffy.

A high-sided tin helps the rolls rise up instead of
out, giving you that pull-apart texture.

These freeze really well, just defrost and reheat in
a warm oven.

For garlic butter, stir a little crushed garlic and
chopped parsley into your melted butter.

     Enriched & Flavoured Breads

CHOCOLATE CHIP VIENNOISES

These soft, enriched mini rolls dotted with chocolate chips take me right back to school – they were always my favourite thing to take with me. Viennoises are a bit like a cross between brioche and pain au lait: lightly sweet, gently enriched, and perfect for breakfast or snacking. I shape them into mini baguettes, just like the ones I used to have as a child.

Prep time: 25 minutes (plus 1 hour 30 minutes resting, or overnight)
| Bake time: 20–25 minutes | Makes: 8 mini rolls

200ml lukewarm milk

30g unsalted butter, softened

15g caster sugar

1 egg

340g strong white bread flour

5g fine salt

7g instant yeast

80g chocolate chips (dark or milk)

For the egg wash

1 egg

2 tbsp double cream

1 tbsp honey

Make the Dough

In a bowl, whisk together the milk, softened butter, sugar, and egg. Add the flour, salt, and yeast. Mix until a dough forms and then knead for 8–10 minutes until smooth and elastic. Gently knead in the chocolate chips.

Cover and let rise for 1–1½ hours at room temperature, or for deeper flavour, chill the dough overnight in the fridge. If chilled, let the dough come to room temperature before shaping.

Shape

Turn the dough onto a floured surface and divide into 8 equal pieces. Roll each piece into a small oval or mini baguette shape, about 12cm long. Place on a lined tray with space between.

Final Rise

Cover loosely and let rise for 30–40 minutes, until puffed.

Bake

Preheat the oven to 180°C fan. Brush the rolls with egg wash mixture, then bake for 20–25 minutes, or until golden brown and just firm on top.

Serve

Best served slightly warm, so the chocolate will be soft and melty inside.

Tips for Success

A slow, overnight rise in the fridge gives deeper flavour and makes the dough easier to work with.

These freeze beautifully once baked and cooled, just defrost and warm through in the microwave for a few seconds until soft.

THYME & CHEDDAR SCONES

I love a savoury bake that's not trying too hard. These little squares are packed with melty cheese and fresh thyme, with a golden top and that classic crackly nigella seed finish. They're the kind of thing you can bake in the morning and eat all day. Every time I make them, I wonder why I don't bake savoury scones more often.

Prep time: 15 minutes | Bake time: 20 minutes | Makes: 8 squares

425g plain flour

2 tsp baking powder

½ tsp fine salt

100g cold unsalted butter, cubed

150g mature cheddar, grated

1 tbsp fresh thyme leaves (or 1 tsp dried)

225ml whole milk + squeeze of lemon juice

1 egg, beaten (for brushing)

1 tsp nigella seeds (for sprinkling)

Make the Dough

In a large bowl, whisk together the flour, baking powder, and salt. Add the butter and rub it in with your fingertips until you have a coarse, sandy texture. Stir in the cheddar and thyme until evenly mixed.

Bring it Together

Pour in the milk and lemon juice and mix with a fork. Once the dough starts coming together, gently knead with your hands until just combined. It should be soft but not sticky.

Shape and Cut

Turn the dough out onto a floured surface and shape into a rectangle about 3cm thick. Use a sharp knife to cut into small chunky squares and place them on a lined baking tray.

Bake

Preheat the oven to 180°C fan. Brush the tops with beaten egg and sprinkle with nigella seeds. Bake for 20 minutes or until golden and the cheese has melted and bubbled at the edges.

Tips for Success

Use a strong cheddar – the flavour really carries the bake.

Don't overwork the dough or the scones will be tough.

Nigella seeds add an earthy crunch on top, but you can swap in sesame if you prefer.

Enriched & Flavoured Breads

PISTACHIO & RASPBERRY DOUGHNUTS

Pistachio and raspberry is one of those flavour combos I'll always come back to. It reminds me of the very first thing I baked in the tent on Bake Off, a pistachio and raspberry cake. These doughnuts are a more playful version of that memory: soft, sugar-coated, and filled with a swirl of pistachio cream and raspberry jam. They look fancy but they're actually so simple to make, for no-fuss, bakery-style doughnuts with the dreamiest filling.

Prep time: 30 minutes (plus 1 hour 30 minutes resting) | Bake time: 20 minutes | Makes: 8 filled doughnuts

For the Dough

175ml warm milk

60g unsalted butter, melted

1 egg

1 tsp vanilla extract

30g caster sugar

7g instant yeast

380g strong white bread flour

10g fine salt

For the Pistachio Cream Filling

30g pistachios

1 tsp neutral oil (sunflower or light olive oil)

100g white chocolate, chopped

80ml double cream

To Finish

Caster sugar (for rolling)

Raspberry jam or compote (for filling)

Extra crushed pistachios (for topping)

Make the Dough

In a large bowl, whisk together the milk, melted butter, egg, vanilla, sugar, and yeast. Add the flour and salt, and mix until a rough dough forms. Knead for 8–10 minutes until smooth and elastic – it might feel sticky at first but will come together as you knead. Cover and let rise for 1 hour or until doubled in size.

Make the Pistachio Cream

In a food processor, blend the pistachios with a teaspoon of oil until smooth and creamy, scraping down the sides as needed to help it along.

Heat the cream until steaming, then pour over the chopped white chocolate. Let sit for 30 seconds, then stir until smooth. Stir in the pistachio paste until fully combined. Chill slightly – the mixture will thicken as it cools.

Shape

Once the dough has risen, punch it down and divide into 8 equal pieces. Roll each one into a smooth ball and place on a tray lined with baking paper, leaving space between. Flatten slightly, cover loosely, and let rise for 30 minutes until puffy.

Fry

Heat oil in a deep pan to 180°C. Fry 2–3 doughnuts at a time for about 1–2 minutes per side, or until golden brown. Remove with a slotted spoon and drain on kitchen paper.

Coat and Fill

While still warm, roll the doughnuts in caster sugar. Let cool slightly before filling.

Use a piping bag fitted with a round nozzle to poke a small hole in the side of each doughnut. Fill generously with pistachio cream and raspberry jam, either swirled together or side by side. Finish with a pinch of crushed pistachios on top.

Tips for Success

Blend the pistachios until glossy and smooth – be patient, it takes a minute.

Let the cream cool slightly before piping to avoid runny filling.

Fry on medium heat – too hot and they brown before cooking through, too low and they go greasy. 180°C is perfect.

SWEET POTATO BURGER BUNS

These are a little twist on classic brioche buns: light, golden, and subtly sweet from mashed sweet potato in the dough. I use my brioche dough from the Foundations chapter as the base, with a little adjustment to the flour to keep things pillowy but still easy to shape. Topped with sesame seeds, these are the buns that make your burgers look (and taste) extra special.

Prep time: 25 minutes (plus 2 hours resting) | Bake time: 20–25 minutes | Makes: 6 buns

200ml lukewarm milk

30g unsalted butter, softened

15g caster sugar

100g mashed sweet potato (from about 1 small sweet potato, steamed or roasted)

375g strong white bread flour

5g fine salt

7g instant yeast

To Finish

1 egg (for egg wash)

2 tbsp sesame seeds

Make the Dough

In a bowl, whisk together the milk, softened butter, sugar, and mashed sweet potato until smooth. Add the flour, salt, and yeast. Mix until a dough forms, then knead for 8–10 minutes until soft, smooth, and slightly tacky.

Rest the Dough

Place the dough in a clean bowl, cover, and let rise for 1 hour 30 minutes or until doubled in size.

Shape

Turn the dough out onto a floured surface and divide into 6 equal pieces. Shape each one into a smooth, round bun and place them on a lined baking tray, spaced apart.

Final Rise

Cover loosely and leave to rise for 30–40 minutes until puffy.

Bake

Preheat the oven to 180°C fan. Brush the buns with beaten egg and sprinkle with sesame seeds. Bake for 20–25 minutes, or until golden and shiny.

Serve

Let cool slightly before slicing. Perfect for burgers, sandwiches, or dipping into soup.

Tips for Success

Roast or steam the sweet potato and mash it well before using – make sure there are no lumps!

These buns are best on the day they're made, but also freeze beautifully.

For extra flavour, try brushing the tops with melted butter as they come out of the oven.

RASPBERRY SCONES

These are the scones I make when I want something that feels a little special but takes almost no effort. The dough is buttery and soft, and the raspberries add just the right amount of tart-sweet fruitiness. I cut them into big chunky triangles, brush the tops with cream and sugar so they bake up golden and crisp, then finish with a simple vanilla glaze. They taste like something from a café but made in your own kitchen – the best kind of baking.

Prep time: 15 minutes | Bake time: 20 minutes | Makes: 8

425g plain flour

2 tsp baking powder

1 tbsp caster sugar

100g cold unsalted butter, cubed

100g fresh or frozen raspberries

225ml whole milk + squeeze of lemon juice

A splash of double cream (for brushing)

1 tbsp demerara or coarse sugar (for sprinkling)

For the Glaze

60g icing sugar

2 tbsp milk

½ tsp vanilla extract

Make the Dough

In a large bowl, whisk together the flour, baking powder, and sugar. Rub in the butter using your fingertips until the mixture resembles coarse breadcrumbs. Add the raspberries and toss gently to coat.

Bring it Together

Pour in the milk with lemon juice and mix with a fork until just combined. Use your hands to gently bring the dough together – it will be soft and slightly sticky.

Shape and Cut

Turn the dough onto a floured surface and shape it into a thick circle, about 4cm tall. Slice into 8 wedges and place them on a lined baking tray.

Bake

Preheat the oven to 180°C fan. Brush the tops with cream and sprinkle with demerara sugar. Bake for 20 minutes, or until golden and risen. Cool on the tray.

Finish

Whisk together the icing sugar, milk, and vanilla, then drizzle over the cooled scones.

Tips for Success

Use frozen raspberries straight from the freezer so they don't bleed too much.

Handle the dough gently to keep the scones light and crumbly.

Don't skip the sugar sprinkle – it gives that classic bakery-style crunch on top.

Enriched & Flavoured Breads

PÂTISSERIE & PASTRIES

Flaky, buttery, and elegant bakes

An introduction to laminated doughs, choux pastry, and delicate pâtisserie-style bakes. Recipes are structured to build confidence, starting with simpler pastries before moving into croissants and more refined techniques.

ZA'ATAR & HARISSA CHEESE TWISTS

These are the kind of pastries I always wish bakeries sold more of – golden, flaky, full of flavour, and a little bit spicy. I use my Rough Puff Pastry from the Foundations chapter (p.24) as the base. A quick spread of harissa, a handful of cheese, and a sprinkle of za'atar turns the dough into these crispy, savoury twists. Serve them warm with soup or as a snack – they never last long!

Prep time: 20 minutes (plus 15 minutes chilling if needed) | Bake time: 15–18 minutes | Makes: 6–8 twists

1 batch rough puff pastry (p.24)

2–3 tbsp harissa paste

100g grated cheese (cheddar, mozzarella, or a mix)

2 tbsp za'atar

1 egg, for egg wash

Sesame or nigella seeds (optional, for topping)

Prepare the Dough

Roll out the chilled pastry into a large rectangle, about 3–4mm thick.

Add the Filling

Spread a thin layer of harissa paste over half the dough. Sprinkle over the cheese and za'atar. Fold the dough in half to sandwich the filling.

Shape the Twists

Cut the folded dough into strips, about 2cm wide. Twist each strip a few times and place on a lined baking tray. Chill for 10–15 minutes if the dough is soft.

Bake

Preheat the oven to 200°C fan. Brush with egg wash and sprinkle with sesame or nigella seeds if using. Bake for 15–18 minutes, or until puffed and golden brown.

Tips for Success

Chill the twists before baking to help them hold their shape.

Don't overload the filling – a light hand keeps the layers defined.

These are best eaten warm, but can be reheated in the oven.

CARAMELISED ONION & MUSHROOM QUICHE

I first had a quiche like this on a brunch date with my mum, and we both couldn't believe how good it was. I'd always thought I didn't like quiche but this one completely changed my mind. The caramelised onions, mushrooms, and cheese make it rich, savoury, and comforting. I use my Shortcrust Pastry from the Foundations chapter (p.22), but without the sugar – a small tweak that makes it perfect for this and lots of other savoury bakes.

Prep time: 30 minutes (plus 40 minutes chilling) | Bake time: 50–55 minutes | Makes: 1 | Serves: 6–8)

For the Pastry

375g plain flour

200g cold unsalted butter, cubed

75ml milk

For the Filling

1 tsp olive oil

1 red onion, finely sliced

1 tsp brown sugar

100g chestnut mushrooms, chopped

½ tsp salt

½ tsp black pepper

½ tsp ground cumin

2 eggs

100ml double cream

40g cheddar cheese, grated

25g grated Parmesan (plus extra for topping)

Make the Pastry

In a large bowl, rub the flour and butter together with your fingertips until it looks like breadcrumbs. Slowly add the milk and bring the dough together – don't overmix. Shape into a disc, wrap, and chill for at least 30 minutes.

Caramelise the Onions

Heat the oil in a pan over low heat and cook the onions for 10–15 minutes, stirring often. Add the brown sugar halfway through to help them caramelise. Stir in the mushrooms and cook for another 5–7 minutes. Season with salt, pepper, and cumin, then set aside to cool slightly.

Make the Filling

In a bowl, whisk the eggs with the double cream. Stir in the cheeses, then fold through the cooled onion and mushroom mixture.

Blind Bake the Pastry

Roll out the chilled pastry and press into a 23cm tart tin. Trim the edges, prick the base with a fork, and chill for 10 minutes. Preheat the oven to 180°C fan. Line with baking paper and fill with baking beans or uncooked rice – this is called blind baking and helps the base cook evenly without puffing up. Bake for 15 minutes, remove the paper and beans, and bake for another 5 minutes until lightly golden.

Fill and Bake

Pour in the filling, sprinkle extra cheese on top, and bake for 25–30 minutes or until golden and set. Let it cool slightly before slicing.

Tips for Success

Chill the pastry before rolling for a flakier texture.

Use mature cheddar for the best flavour kick.

Let the onion mixture cool before adding to the cream so it doesn't scramble the eggs.

Pâtisserie & Pastries

APRICOT & STRAWBERRY GALETTE

This is one of my go-to summer bakes – easy, forgiving, and always impressive. I make it on repeat every year.
You can use any fruit you have (fresh or frozen), and it still turns out beautifully. Best served warm with a scoop
of ice cream.

Prep time: 15 minutes (plus 30 minutes chilling) | Bake time: 30–35 minutes | Makes: 1 medium galette | Serves: 6

For the Pastry

75g cold unsalted butter, cubed

150g plain flour

40g caster sugar

25ml cold milk

For the Filling

Fruit of choice (try apricots, strawberries, frozen
berries, plums, nectarines)

For Brushing

3 tbsp milk

1 tbsp runny honey

Turbinado or demerara sugar, for sprinkling

Make the Pastry

In a bowl, rub the cold butter into the flour and sugar using your fingertips until the
mixture resembles fine crumbs. Add the milk and gently bring the dough together.
Flatten into a disc, wrap, and chill for 30 minutes.

Shape and Fill

Roll the chilled pastry between two sheets of baking paper into a rough circle (about
3–4mm thick). Arrange your fruit in the centre, leaving a 2–3 inch border.
Fold the edges of the pastry up over the fruit, pleating as you go. It's meant to look
rustic!

Brush and Bake

Mix the milk and honey together and brush over the folded pastry edges. Sprinkle
generously with turbinado sugar.
Bake at 160°C fan for 30–35 minutes, or until golden brown and bubbling.
Cool slightly and serve warm with ice cream.

Tips for Success

Don't worry about making the pastry perfect –
galettes are meant to be rustic.
Chill the dough to help it roll out neatly and
bake up crisp.
Turbinado or demerara sugar gives the edges a
crunchy golden finish.

CLASSIC APPLE PIE

There's nothing like the smell of freshly baked apple pie filling the house. This apple pie is the ultimate comfort food thanks to its perfectly spiced apple filling, buttery crust, and golden, crisp top. It's my go-to recipe for any occasion and always a crowd-pleaser. Whether it's for a special gathering or a cosy weekend dessert, this pie never fails to impress!

Prep time: 35 minutes | Bake time: 35–40 minutes | Serves: 8

For the Filling

6 medium Granny Smith apples, peeled, cored and sliced

125g soft light brown sugar

2½ tsp ground cinnamon

1 tsp ground nutmeg

3 tbsp cornflour

4 tbsp cold water

For the Pastry

375g plain flour

100g caster sugar

200g cold butter, cubed

75ml milk

To Finish

Milk, for brushing on top before baking

Demerara sugar, for sprinkling

Make the Filling

Place the sliced apples in a pot with the brown sugar, cinnamon, and nutmeg. Mix well and cook over medium heat, stirring often. Once it starts bubbling, dissolve the cornflour in the cold water and add it to the apples.

Continue cooking until the filling thickens, then transfer to a bowl and chill.

Prepare the Pastry

In a large bowl, mix the flour, caster sugar, and butter. Use your fingertips to rub the butter into the flour until the mixture resembles breadcrumbs. You can also do this in a food processer.

Add the milk and bring the dough together. Split it into two halves, then place each half between two sheets of parchment paper and roll out the dough, ensuring it's thin enough for a crisp pie crust (about 3mm thick). The parchment paper prevents sticking and makes it easier to roll out evenly.

Assemble the Pie

Line an 8-inch tart tin with one half of the rolled-out pastry. Trim the excess by rolling the rolling pin across the top of the tin.

Pour the chilled apple filling into the pastry base and spread to the edges.

Decorate and Bake

Roll out the remaining pastry and cut into strips. For the lattice, lay half of the strips over the pie with space in between them. Fold back every other strip and place a new strip across the flat strips. Bring the folded strips back down, then repeat, alternating the folded strips each time. Continue until the pie is covered.

Bake in a preheated oven at 160°C fan for 35–40 minutes, or until golden brown.

Tips for Success

Ensure your butter is cold for a flakier pastry.

Chill the apple filling before adding it to the crust to prevent sogginess.

APPLE & PEAR TARTE TATIN

A classic French tart flipped upside-down after baking the soft, caramelised fruit layered under crisp, buttery pastry. I like to shape mine like a flower: pears arranged like petals, with a whole apple half in the centre. It's surprisingly simple, and the pastry base is the same one I use for my galette. Serve it warm with ice cream or crème fraîche.

Prep time: 30 minutes (plus 30 minutes chilling) | Bake time: 40–45 minutes | Makes: 1 tart | Serves: 6–8

For the Pastry

75g cold unsalted butter, cubed

150g plain flour

40g caster sugar

25ml cold milk

For the Fruit and Caramel

60g unsalted butter

80g caster sugar

3 firm pears, peeled, halved, and cored

1 small apple, peeled, halved, and cored

Make the Pastry

In a bowl, rub the butter into the flour and sugar with your fingertips. Add the milk and bring the dough together. Wrap and chill for 30 minutes.

Prepare the Caramel and Fruit

In a 20–22cm oven-safe pan or tart tin, melt the butter and sugar over medium heat. Let it bubble without stirring until it turns into a golden caramel (watch closely so it doesn't burn).

Remove from the heat and arrange the pear halves cut-side down in a circular pattern, with the apple half in the centre like a flower.

Place the pan in the oven and bake for 10–15 minutes to soften the fruit slightly and deepen the caramel.

Top with Pastry

Roll out the chilled pastry into a circle slightly larger than your pan. Carefully lay it over the softened fruit and tuck the edges in. Prick the top a few times with a fork.

Bake

Bake at 180°C fan for 25–30 minutes, or until the pastry is golden and crisp.

Flip and Serve

Cool for 5 minutes, then place a large plate over the tart and carefully flip it out. The fruit should be glossy and caramelised. Serve warm with cream or ice cream.

Tips for Success

Don't rush the caramel – a deep golden colour gives the best flavour.

Use firm pears so they hold their shape after baking.

Flip while still warm so the caramel doesn't set in the pan.

Pâtisserie & Pastries

MIXED BERRY TART

This tart reminds me why I love simple bakes. It looks like something you'd see in a bakery window, but it's made with the same easy pastry I use for my Apricot & Strawberry Galette (p.162). The filling is a soft, silky vanilla crème mousseline that holds everything together without feeling heavy. I like to pile it with whatever berries I've got, and it always turns out delicious. It's the kind of dessert that feels like a treat without trying too hard.

Prep time: 35 minutes (plus 30 minutes chilling) | Bake time: 20–25 minutes | Makes: 1 tart | Serves: 6–8

For the Pastry

75g cold unsalted butter, cubed

150g plain flour

40g caster sugar

25ml cold milk

For the Crème Mousseline Filling

240ml whole milk

40g caster sugar

½ tsp vanilla paste

3 egg yolks

40g caster sugar (second quantity)

2 tbsp cornflour

2 tbsp plain flour

150g unsalted butter, softened

To Finish

Fresh mixed berries (strawberries, raspberries, blackberries, blueberries)

Icing sugar, for dusting (optional)

Make the Pastry

Rub the butter into the flour and sugar using your fingertips. Add the milk and bring the dough together. Flatten into a disc, wrap, and chill for 30 minutes.

Roll out the chilled dough and press into a tart tin (20–22cm). Trim the edges and prick the base with a fork. Chill for another 15 minutes.

Blind Bake

Preheat the oven to 180°C fan. Line the tart shell with baking paper and fill with baking beans or uncooked rice. Bake for 15 minutes, then remove the paper and beans. Bake for another 8–10 minutes until golden. Let cool completely.

Make the Crème Mousseline

In a saucepan, heat the milk, 40g sugar, and vanilla until steaming.

In a separate bowl, whisk the egg yolks and the second 40g of sugar until light. Add the cornflour and flour and mix well.

Slowly pour the hot milk into the egg mixture while whisking. Return everything to the saucepan and cook over medium heat, whisking constantly until thick and smooth.

Transfer to a bowl, cover with cling film (touching the surface), and chill completely. Once cool, beat in the softened butter until pale, smooth, and creamy.

Assemble the Tart

Spoon the crème mousseline into the cooled tart shell and smooth the surface. Pile the fresh berries on top. Chill for 10–15 minutes before serving, or serve immediately with a dusting of icing sugar.

Tips for Success

Don't skip chilling the pastry, it helps keep the shell crisp and neat.

This tart is best eaten the same day, but leftovers keep well chilled for up to 2 days.

Pâtisserie & Pastries

RASPBERRY FINANCIERS

Soft, buttery, and golden with crisp edges – these little French almond cakes are one of my favourite ways to use up egg whites. Traditionally made with ground almonds and browned butter, I bake them in mini tartlet tins which gives them the prettiest scalloped edges. The raspberries add a juicy burst that cuts through the sweetness and makes them feel a little fancy, even though they're super easy to make. Perfect for teatime or a quick bake when you've got spare berries lying around.

Prep time: 15 minutes | Bake time: 18–20 minutes | Makes: 6–8 mini tartlets

100g unsalted butter

100g icing sugar

35g plain flour

90g ground almonds

¼ tsp salt

3 egg whites (90–100g)

½ tsp vanilla extract (optional)

Fresh raspberries

Flaked almonds (optional)

Brown the Butter

Place the butter in a small pan over medium heat. Let it melt, then cook gently until the solids at the bottom turn golden and it smells nutty. Remove from the heat and set aside to cool slightly.

Mix the Dry Ingredients

In a bowl, whisk together the icing sugar, plain flour, ground almonds, and salt.

Add the Wet Ingredients

Whisk the egg whites until frothy (no need to whip). Add to the dry ingredients along with the vanilla (if using), then pour in the browned butter. Stir until smooth and well combined.

Bake

Divide the mixture between lightly greased mini tartlet tins, filling each about three-quarters full. Gently press a raspberry into the centre of each. Sprinkle with flaked almonds if using.

Bake at 180°C fan for 18–20 minutes, or until golden around the edges and just set in the middle. Leave to cool slightly before removing from the tins.

Tips for Success

Browning the butter brings out so much extra flavour and is so worth the tiny bit of effort.

No tartlet tins? A mini muffin tray works too.

ORANGE BLOSSOM LEMON POSSET

This is probably the simplest recipe in the whole book, but it deserves its place. The texture is so creamy, the flavour is bright and floral, and it sets like magic with just a few ingredients. It's the kind of thing you'd expect on a fancy restaurant menu, but it takes minutes to make. I love serving it in lemon shells, but any small glass or ramekin works too.

Prep time: 10 minutes (plus 4 hours or overnight chilling) | Bake time: 5 minutes | Makes: 2–3 small portions

200ml double cream

50g caster sugar

30ml fresh lemon juice

1 tsp orange blossom water

Heat the Cream

In a small saucepan, combine the cream and sugar. Bring to a gentle simmer over medium heat and let it bubble for 2–3 minutes, stirring occasionally. Don't let it boil too rapidly, just enough to dissolve the sugar and reduce slightly.

Add Flavour

Remove from the heat. Stir in the lemon juice and orange blossom water. It should thicken slightly as the acid reacts with the cream.

Chill

Pour into lemon shells, ramekins, or small glasses. Cool to room temperature, then chill for at least 4 hours (or overnight) until set.

Serve

Top with lemon zest, edible flowers, or a little shortbread on the side.

Tips for Success

Don't skip the simmer – the heat is what allows it to set properly.

The orange blossom is optional but adds such a lovely flavour!

These keep well in the fridge for 2–3 days.

CROISSANTS

Flaky, buttery, and crisp on the outside, homemade croissants are a labour of love, but the results are well worth the effort. This recipe builds on my Bakery-Style Flaky Pastry (p.26) from the Foundations chapter, so be sure to prepare that first.

Prep time: 30 minutes (plus 2–3 hours proving) | Bake time: 20–25 minutes | Makes: 8 croissants

1 batch chilled Bakery-Style Flaky Pastry (p.26)

1 medium egg

30ml double cream

Shape the Croissants

Continuing from the Shape and Fill step of my flaky pastry recipe, roll the chilled dough into a 5mm-thick rectangle (40 x 30cm).

Cut into eight long triangles (approx. 6cm wide at the base), using a zig-zag pattern from edge to edge to create even shapes.

Roll each triangle from the wide end to the tip, gently stretching as you roll to create the classic croissant shape.

Prove and Bake

Place the croissants on a lined baking tray, spacing them apart so they have room to rise.

Let them prove at room temperature for 2–3 hours until puffed up and jiggly.

Whisk together the egg and double cream for the egg wash, then brush it over the croissants.

Bake at 180°C fan for 20–25 minutes, or until deep golden brown.

Tips for Success

Lamination works best when everything stays cold. If the butter starts to soften at any stage, pop the dough back into the fridge to chill before continuing.

Proving temperature matters: too warm and the butter may melt; too cool, and the dough won't rise properly. Aim for around 22–24°C. If your kitchen is colder, prove in a switched-off oven with the light on.

When rolling the croissants, don't press too hard. Gently stretch the dough as you roll for a better rise and an even, flaky structure.

Properly proved croissants should look puffy, feel light, and have a slight wobble when you shake the tray. If they feel dense, give them more time to prove before baking.

Brush a light layer of egg wash before proving, then a second layer just before baking for a deep, golden shine.

Pâtisserie & Pastries

ALMOND CROISSANTS

This is my go-to way of turning day-old croissants into something even better. A simple almond filling, a quick sugar syrup, and a sprinkle of flaked almonds – it's honestly bakery-level with barely any effort. You can use the croissant recipe from earlier in this chapter, or shop-bought ones work just as well. They're best served warm, when the filling is soft and the tops are golden and crisp.

Prep time: 15 minutes | Bake time: 15 minutes | Makes: 4 filled croissants

For the Frangipane Filling

75g unsalted butter, softened

50g caster sugar

75g ground almonds

1 egg

½ tsp almond extract

For the Syrup

25g caster sugar

50ml water

To Finish

4 croissants (preferably a day old)

Flaked almonds

Icing sugar, to dust

Make the Filling

In a bowl, mix the softened butter, sugar, and ground almonds until you have a smooth paste. Add the egg and almond extract and beat until fully combined. Set aside.

Make the Syrup

In a small pan, heat the sugar and water until the sugar has dissolved. Set aside to cool slightly.

Assemble the Croissants

Slice each croissant in half. Brush both the cut sides with sugar syrup. Pipe or spoon some frangipane into the middle, then sandwich the tops back on. Spread a little more frangipane over the top and sprinkle with flaked almonds.

Bake

Place the filled croissants on a lined tray and bake at 160°C fan for 10–15 minutes, or until golden and crisp on top.

Serve

Dust with icing sugar and serve warm.

Tips for Success

This recipe works best with croissants that are a day or two old – they'll hold their shape better and soak up the syrup without going soggy.

You can prep them ahead and bake to serve, perfect for easy breakfasts or brunch.

Pâtisserie & Pastries

PISTACHIO CROISSANTS

These croissants will always hold a special place in my heart – they're the ones that got me into Bake Off. I baked a batch the night before my audition, filled them with my signature creamy pistachio filling, and carried them on the train hoping they'd survive the journey. They did, and the judges loved them. If you've made croissants from scratch (p.174), this is the perfect way to turn them into something extra special.

Prep time: 15 minutes | Makes: 4 filled croissants

4 fresh croissants (homemade or bakery-bought)

For the Pistachio Filling
50g pistachios
2 tbsp neutral oil
100g white chocolate, melted
40ml double cream

To Finish
Extra crushed pistachios
Icing sugar (optional)

Make the Filling

Blend the pistachios with the oil in a food processor until smooth and creamy. In a bowl, combine the melted white chocolate and double cream, then stir in the pistachio paste. Mix until smooth and glossy. Transfer to a piping bag.

Fill the Croissants

Use a sharp knife to make a small hole in the side or base of each croissant. Pipe the pistachio cream inside until they feel nicely filled.

Top and Decorate

Pipe a little extra pistachio cream over the top of each croissant, then sprinkle with crushed pistachios.

Serve

Best enjoyed fresh, ideally slightly warm so the filling is soft and creamy.

Tips for Success

Use toasted pistachios for the filling – it brings out a deeper, nuttier flavour.

Let the filling cool slightly before piping so it thickens and holds inside the croissant.

The filling keeps well in the fridge for a few days – just bring it back to room temp before using.

EASY PAIN AU CHOCOLAT

This is the recipe I shared a few years ago on my page that ended up reaching millions, and it's still one of the easiest ways to make flaky, buttery pastries at home. You don't need a butter block or any fancy equipment. Just your hands, cold butter, and a few gentle folds, using a variation of my Rough Puff Pastry from the Foundations chapter (p.24). This version is perfect for beginners!

Prep time: 30 minutes (plus 1 hour 30 minutes chilling and 1–2 hours proving)
| Bake time: 20–25 minutes | Makes: 6–8 pastries

250g strong white bread flour

20g caster sugar

5g fine salt

7g instant yeast

180g cold unsalted butter, cubed

120ml cold water or milk

For the Filling

1 bar milk or dark chocolate, cut into strips

For the Egg Wash

1 egg

1 tbsp double cream

1 tbsp honey

Make the Dough

In a large bowl, combine the flour, sugar, salt, and yeast. Add the cold cubed butter and rub it in gently – you want to keep some visible pieces of butter. Pour in the cold water or milk and stir until the dough just comes together. Don't knead. Wrap and chill for 15 minutes.

Roll and Fold

On a lightly floured surface, roll the dough into a rectangle. Fold the top third down, then the bottom third up over it (like folding a letter). Turn the dough 90° and repeat the fold once more. Chill for 10–15 minutes.

Repeat the same fold one more time (3 folds total), then wrap and chill the dough for 1 hour.

Shape and Fill

Roll the chilled dough into a large rectangle, about 3–4mm thick. Trim the edges, then cut into smaller rectangles for your pain au chocolat.

Place 1–2 strips of chocolate near one short edge of each rectangle. Roll up tightly, sealing the seam underneath. Place on a lined tray, seam side down.

Egg Wash

Mix the egg, cream, and honey for the egg wash.

Prove

Brush the pastries lightly with egg wash then cover loosely with cling film and let prove in a warm place for 1–2 hours, or until noticeably puffed.

Bake

Once proved, give them a second coat of egg wash for a deeper colour. Bake at 200°C fan for 20–25 minutes, or until golden and crisp.

Tips for Success

Don't overwork the dough: those visible bits of butter = flake.

Keep everything cold throughout folding and shaping.

Use two chocolate strips per pastry for the classic bakery-style finish.

RASPBERRY & CUSTARD
DANISH

This one's inspired by a Danish I picked up at a bakery once and couldn't stop thinking about – crisp, flaky layers, soft vanilla custard in the centre, and a burst of raspberry on top. I use my go-to laminated dough for this, it's a bit of a project, but so worth it. The end result is proper bakery style pastry at home.

Prep time: 1 hour (plus 4 hours or overnight chilling and 1–2 hours proving)
| Bake time: 20–25 minutes | Makes: 8–10 pastries

For the Dough

100ml lukewarm water

7g instant yeast

1 medium egg (plus extra for the egg wash)

250g strong white bread flour

30g caster sugar

5g fine salt

10g skimmed milk powder

30g unsalted butter, softened

180g cold unsalted butter (for laminating)

For the Vanilla Pastry Cream

150ml whole milk

20g caster sugar

½ tsp vanilla paste

2 egg yolks

20g caster sugar (second quantity)

2 tbsp cornflour

20g unsalted butter, softened

To Finish

Fresh raspberries

Icing sugar, for dusting

Make the Dough

Whisk the water, yeast, and egg in a large bowl. Add the flour, sugar, salt, and milk powder. Mix to combine, then knead in the softened butter until smooth (about 5–7 minutes). Cover and rest for 30 minutes.

Chill the Dough and Butter

Shape the dough into a rectangle, wrap, and chill for 30 minutes. Meanwhile, roll the cold butter between baking paper into a 15 × 20cm block. Chill for 15 minutes.

Laminate the Dough

Roll the dough to twice the size of the butter. Place the butter in the centre, fold the dough over it like an envelope, and seal. Roll into a long rectangle, fold into thirds, then wrap and chill for 30 minutes.

Repeat twice more (for three folds in total), chilling between each fold. After the final fold, rest the dough for 2–3 hours or overnight.

Make the Pastry Cream

Heat the milk, 20g sugar, and vanilla until steaming. In a separate bowl, whisk the egg yolks and remaining sugar until dissolved, then stir in the cornflour. Slowly pour in the hot milk, whisking as you go. Return to the pan and cook over medium heat, whisking constantly until thickened.

Transfer to a bowl, chill completely, then beat in the butter until smooth and pale.

Shape and Fill

Roll the dough to 5mm thick and cut into ovals or circles. Cover loosely with cling film and prove for 1–2 hours, until puffy. Use a small lid or the base of a glass to gently press the centre. Pipe pastry cream into the indent and top with a few raspberries.

Bake

Preheat the oven to 180°C fan. Brush the exposed pastry with egg wash and bake for 20–25 minutes, or until golden and flaky. Cool slightly, then dust with icing sugar.

Tips for Success

Keep everything cold for clean, flaky layers.

Pâtisserie & Pastries

CHOUX AU CRAQUELIN WITH HAZELNUT CHANTILLY CREAM

These little choux puffs feel like something you'd find in a Parisian pâtisserie, but they're so doable at home. The craquelin bakes into a delicate, crisp topping, and inside is a dreamy whipped hazelnut cream. I like to finish them with a swirl of plain Chantilly and a few edible flowers to make them even more delicate, elegant, and honestly, so fun to make.

Prep time: 35 minutes (plus chilling) | Bake time: 25–30 minutes | Makes: 8–10

For the Craquelin Topping

50g unsalted butter, softened

60g light brown sugar

60g plain flour

For the Choux Pastry

75g unsalted butter

60ml water

Pinch of salt

1 tsp sugar

75g plain flour

2 medium eggs, beaten

For the Hazelnut Chantilly Cream

250ml double cream

2 tbsp icing sugar

1–2 tbsp hazelnut spread

½ tsp vanilla paste

Make the Craquelin

Mix the butter, sugar, and flour in a small bowl until a dough forms. Roll it out between two sheets of baking paper to about 2–3mm thick. Freeze until firm, then cut into circles (about the size of your piped choux).

Make the Choux

Add the butter, water, salt, and sugar to a saucepan and bring to a simmer. Once the butter melts, remove from the heat and stir in the flour all at once. Mix until it forms a ball and pulls away from the sides.

Return to low heat for 1–2 minutes to cook off some moisture. Let cool for 5 minutes, then gradually mix in the eggs. You want a smooth, pipeable dough that holds its shape.

Pipe and Bake

Preheat the oven to 180°C fan.

Pipe the dough into blobs (about 4cm wide) onto a lined baking tray.

Top each with a craquelin circle.

Bake for 25–30 minutes until puffed and golden. Cool completely.

Make the Chantilly Cream

Whip the double cream, icing sugar, hazelnut spread, and vanilla until it holds soft peaks. Transfer to a piping bag with a small round nozzle.

Fill and Decorate

Use a small knife or skewer to poke a hole in the base of each choux. Pipe in the hazelnut cream.

This is optional but you can top with an extra swirl of plain Chantilly cream (or more hazelnut cream if you like) and finish with edible flowers.

Tips for Success

Keep everything cold when whipping cream, it helps it hold better.

If you don't have hazelnut spread, you can use pistachio or chocolate spread instead.

These are best eaten the same day, but you can make the shells ahead and fill just before serving.

ACKNOWLEDGEMENTS

Writing this book has been one of the most challenging, rewarding and emotional projects of my life, and it wouldn't exist without the love and encouragement I've received along the way.

To my family, who have always believed in me, even when I doubted myself: thank you for every taste test, every dish you cleaned behind me and every "yes" when I needed it most. **Mum**, your strength and gentleness are in every page. I hope this book makes you proud. To my little sister **Juri**, the joy of my life and the one who looks up to me as her older sister – I wrote this book for you. Thank you for being one of my biggest supporters and for even sharing the news about my cookbook with your whole school. Ahh, I love you. To my **dad**, thank you for the late-night drives to pick up last-minute ingredients I'd forgotten for recipe tests and for witnessing just how much butter and flour went into this book. To my brothers **Mohammed** and **Moataz**, I hope you're proud of your sister. Thank you for supporting me through all my indecisiveness, from choosing the book cover to finalising the bakes.

To my best friends **Noor** and **Zahra**, thank you for being some of the first to hear about this book, for being there from day one and getting all the updates, for picnics and pep talks, and for never getting tired of cookie trials or focaccia reels. Thank you for helping with book decisions and for sending me endless inspiration for recipes and ideas for shoots. Your support has meant everything.

To the team at **Meze Publishing**: **Emma**, thank you for your support from day one of this journey; **Paul**, thank you for designing the book and bringing my visual ideas to life; **Emily**, who helped with the initial editing of the recipes, and to the rest of the team who helped with editing the remaining recipes – thank you!

This one deserves a big shoutout – **Ellie**, the talented photographer behind this book. She was so much more than just a photographer; we styled this book together. Thank you for bringing my vision to life. I couldn't have got through the long shoot days without your encouragement and hard work. You really treated this as a personal project. This book holds so many memories, from filling up our tiny cars with props, to driving around to the different shoot locations. Thank you!

My online community – you made this book possible. You've cheered me on through every video, every recipe, and every wobble. I still can't believe something so personal could reach so many people.

Finally, **to anyone holding this book in their hands** – thank you. I hope you make these recipes your own and I hope they bring as much warmth to your kitchen as they have to mine.

CONVERSION CHARTS

WEIGHTS	
METRIC	**IMPERIAL**
15g	½ oz
25g	1 oz
40g	1½ oz
50g	2 oz
75g	3 oz
100g	4 oz
150g	5 oz
175g	6 oz
200g	7 oz
225g	8 oz
250g	9 oz
275g	10 oz
350g	12 oz
375g	13 oz
400g	14 oz
425g	15 oz
450g	1 lb
550g	1¼ lb
675g	1½ lb
900g	2 lb
1.5kg	3 lb
1.75g	4 lb
2.25kg	5 lb

VOLUME	
METRIC	**IMPERIAL**
25ml	1 fl oz
50ml	2 fl oz
85ml	3 fl oz
150ml	5 fl oz (¼ pint)
300ml	10 fl oz (½ pint)
450ml	15 fl oz (¾ pint)
600ml	1 pint
700ml	1¼ pints
900ml	1½ pints
1 litre	1¾ pints
1.2 litres	2 pints
1.25 litres	2¼ pints
1.5 litres	2½ pints
1.6 litres	2¾ pints
1.75 litres	3 pints
1.8 litres	3¼ pints
2 litres	3½ pints
2.1 litres	3¾ pints
2.25 litres	4 pints
2.75 litres	5 pints
3.4 litres	6 pints
3.9 litres	7 pints
5 litres	8 pints (1 gallon)

MEASUREMENTS

METRIC	IMPERIAL
0.5cm	¼ inch
1cm	½ inch
2.5cm	1 inch
5cm	2 inches
7.5cm	3 inches
10cm	4 inches
15cm	6 inches
18cm	7 inches
20cm	8 inches
23cm	9 inches
25cm	10 inches
30cm	12 inches

OVEN TEMPERATURES

°C	°C FAN	°F	GAS MARK
140°C	120°C	275°F	Gas Mark 1
150°C	130°C	300°F	Gas Mark 2
160°C	140°C	325°F	Gas Mark 3
180°C	160°C	350°F	Gas Mark 4
190°C	170°C	375°F	Gas Mark 5
200°C	180°C	400°F	Gas Mark 6
220°C	200°C	425°F	Gas Mark 7
230°C	210°C	450°F	Gas Mark 8
240°C	220°C	475°F	Gas Mark 9